GET THAT NOVEL STARTED
(AND KEEP IT GOING 'TIL YOU FINISH)

GET THAT NOVEL STARTED!

(AND KEEP IT GOING 'TIL YOU FINISH)

DONNA LEVIN

Writer's Digest Books

Cincinnati, Ohio

ABOUT THE AUTHOR

Donna Levin is the author of two novels, *Extraordinary Means* (Arbor House) and *California Street* (Simon & Schuster). She teaches a novel-writing workshop at the University of California at Berkeley extension, and Boston University is including her work in its archives of twentieth-century authors. She lives in San Francisco.

Get That Novel Started! (And Keep It Going 'Til You Finish). Copyright © 1992 by Donna Levin. Printed and bound in the United States of America. All rights reserved. No part of this book may be reproduced in any form or by any electronic or mechanical means including information storage and retrieval systems without permission in writing from the publisher, except by a reviewer, who may quote brief passages in a review. Published by Writer's Digest Books, an imprint of F&W Publications, Inc., 1507 Dana Avenue, Cincinnati, Ohio 45207. First edition.

This hardcover edition of *Get That Novel Started! (And Keep It Going 'Til You Finish)* features a "self-jacket" that eliminates the need for a separate dust jacket. It provides sturdy protection for your book while it saves paper, trees and energy.

96 95 94 93   5 4 3 2

Library of Congress Cataloging in Publication Data

Levin, Donna.
     Get that novel started! (and keep it going 'til you finish) / Donna Levin.
        p.   cm.
Includes index.
     ISBN 0-89879-517-6
1. Fiction—Authorship.   I. Title.
PN3355.L39   1992
808.3—dc20   92-23186
                                                            CIP

Edited by Mark Kissling
Designed by Paul Neff

DEDICATION

For my mother,
Helen Stern Levin,
who gave me stories to tell,
and my father,
Marvin Levin,
who bought me an IBM
and told me to get started.

ACKNOWLEDGMENTS

If writing itself takes a leap of faith, then the people who believe in writers are like astronauts. Here are some of the astronauts I know and love:

First, Chris Olmedo, who with her patience, skill and creativity, has taught my children, William and Sonia, most of what they know. She's taken almost as much care of me as she has of them.

Several fine, hardworking authors took time away from their work to share their experiences: Jack Albin Anderson, Barbara Brooker, Phyllis Burke, James N. Frey, Donna Gillespie and Brad Newsham.

More fine, hardworking authors in my writing group contributed wisdom: Donal Brown, Margaret Cuthbert, Bruce Hartford, Bob Hunt and Leigh Anne Varney.

Suzanne Juergensen, Waimea Williams and John Winch are in another writing group, and I couldn't live without them.

My agent, Gloria Loomis, and her assistant, Kendra Taylor, are Goddesses Who Live in New York.

Bill Brohaugh and Mark Kissling, my editors at Writer's Digest Books, worked long and thoroughly on this manuscript; if it's any good, they get the credit.

Sue Smith, of the University of California at Berkeley extension, and Meera Lester, of Writers Connection, each gave me an opportunity to teach, mostly on my word that I could.

All the sincere, striving folks who have attended my classes and seminars over the years have taught me more than I could ever hope to teach them.

And then there's Michael Bernick, without whom, the deluge.

TABLE OF CONTENTS

We tell ourselves stories in order to live.

Joan Didion, *The White Album*

He's as nervous as a badly abused laboratory animal, first kept awake for too long, periodically electrocuted, then given large doses of dangerous drugs and placed in a maze with no exit. He's a writer.

Anne Lamott, *Joe Jones*

One Girl's Story

An Otherwise Bleak Landscape

When I was thirteen, I stayed up all night one Saturday reading George Orwell's *1984*. It's the story of Winston Smith, an ordinary man who lives in a bleak, futuristic world where there are no freedoms, no luxuries, no privacy and where, ultimately, there is no one to love.

What gripped me that night was the way I could taste, smell and touch all the grimness and loneliness of Winston's life, in Orwell's relentless detailing of inedible food, elevators that never worked, and, especially, the blaring of the telescreen, a two-way television that watches everyone constantly. That I identified so strongly with poor Winston may say something about my own adolescence, but I'll save that for another book.

By the time I got to the part where Winston meets Julia, a woman who falls in love with him, I clung to my paperback copy as if I could read my own future in it. I kept reading, elbows propped on my turquoise bedspread, as early morning light penetrated my venetian blinds and Sunday school loomed. I finished the book just before it was time to get dressed.

That was the night I decided I wanted to be a writer. Look what a writer can accomplish! Orwell had been dead for a long time, but he had just told me a story so moving and unsettling that I would never forget it. (The first line sounds in my head still: "It was a bright cold day in April, and the clocks were striking thirteen. . . .") I wanted to be able to do the same. I wanted, someday, for there to be people staying up to read my books.

Even before that night, I had regarded books as magical objects. Without fancy gadgetry, they travel through time and space: they tell us what our ancestors were like or how people from another culture live. They allow people to sort through and to order their thoughts, and therefore often to express what lies more deeply beneath the surface—to reach nobler and truer emotions than are accessible in casual conversations. Books are the result of years of solitude and meditation; they stand as achievements of the human spirit.

The novel is a particularly admirable feat. Though novelists may use real-life people and events as starting points, they always end up with products of their unique imaginations. Yet Winston Smith, Madame Bovary, Holden Caulfield, Hester Prynne, Raskolnikov, Jake Barnes and all their fictional company are as real and memorable as any person who ever lived. And the story of a good novel resonates within us as something truer than life: Anna Karenina's death, Rhett Butler slamming the door, Oliver Twist's life on the streets, Jay Gatsby's unquestioning love for Daisy. Good fiction is as much a part of our history as the Civil War.

The same year I read *1984*, I read *Gone With the Wind* for the first time. There couldn't be two more different novels, except that both of them made me want to cry from how much I wanted to write them. From then on, no desire would ever lodge itself as deeply in me as becoming a novelist.

Of course, I knew perfectly well that novelists were geniuses, but I was only thirteen, so I thought it might still turn out that I was a genius, too. I imagined the scene. "Some people *have* it," a glazed-eyed instructor would say, whispering in awe, "and *you* have it!"

I did take a couple of creative writing classes in high school and college where I wrote amusing pieces that my friends often liked, but no one ever took me aside to tell me I was destined to become the next F. Scott Fitzgerald.

I also had ideas for novels—vague notions floating in my head like spots before tired eyes. I believed, though, that a truly talented author wrote without effort. If the book were the right book, and I were the right author, it would emerge complete, like Athena bursting from Zeus's head.

But when I occasionally did get around to sitting down at a typewriter (this was back in the Bronze Age when hardly anyone except big law firms had word processors), I didn't like what I wrote. And I soon experienced problems—blank spaces, rough spots. The effort required didn't jive with my belief about how good writers wrote, so I abandoned my attempts each time. After all, there were plenty of other things to keep me occupied: television, movies, meals, phone calls, dishes, shampoos and pedicures.

It is in fact true that not everyone is destined to be a novelist; some of us are better suited to certain professions than others. I doubt that I would make a very good surgeon or fighter pilot. The difference was that I never lay awake at night tortured with thoughts like, "I could be taking out an appendix tomorrow—if only I'd stuck with biology for a second semester!"

As years passed, I drifted away from writing. When I heard stories about my contemporaries who were beginning to succeed as writers, and read reviews of books by authors who were younger than me, the unfulfilled ambition nagged at me—but the prospect of actually beginning a long project was always too overwhelming.

The most persuasive evidence that I should just plain give up came when the author Anne Lamott published her first novel at the tender age of twenty-six. Annie and I had been in the same high school creative writing class, so I liked to think that I could share in her accomplishment, assuming that at some point I had offered her a piece of astute criticism. But I didn't remember any—all I could remember was that she was a terrific writer back in high school, too.

And then I did the math: Considering that fewer than two hundred first novels—sometimes far fewer—are published by major publishers each year, what were the odds that two novelists could come out of a creative writing class of eight? I reminded myself that Barbra Streisand and Neil Diamond went to the same high school in New York, but strangely, that didn't comfort me.

Two Lucky Strikes

Out of equal parts boredom and desperation, I signed up for a writing class at San Francisco State University extension. (I hadn't been in a writing class since college, six years before.) The instructor was primarily a poet, a very different craft from that of the novelist, but she was very gentle and encouraging, and gave my ailing writing ego a much-needed booster shot.

As a result of that class, another lucky thing happened. A student in the class told me about a workshop in Berkeley led by a "brilliant teacher," as she described him, named Leonard Bishop.

I joined his workshop, and it changed my life. (How often do you get to say *that*?) We met every Monday night, fifty-two weeks a year, in the living rooms of different houses. Leonard taught me many important aspects of craft (plot was his favorite subject), but many people could have taught me about craft. Few teachers, I think, can demystify writing and impart to their students the kind of belief in themselves that a writer needs. When I whined and complained (frequently) that I wanted to give up, Leonard simply said, "Don't give up. If you keep writing, you will be published."

Four-and-a-half years after joining Leonard's group, Arbor House (now part of William Morrow), bought my first novel, *Extraordinary Means*.

The Concert Pianist

I can hear you thinking, *Four-and-a-half years? It seems like a long time to me!* Well, sure, it is. But how long do doctors go to medical school? How long does it take to earn a Ph.D.?

There is this myth going around—that I once subscribed to—that if you have writing talent, you simply write, and people fall over at how brilliant your writing is. I have a theory about how this myth arose.

First of all, no one expects a person, no matter how gifted, to walk up to a piano and play a concerto without ever having had a lesson. To play a piano, one must learn to read music and learn which keys correspond to which notes—and that's just for starters.

But virtually all of us already know how to read and write: grocery lists, business letters, checks, clever thank-you notes. Most of us can type, and with a computer you don't even need to type very well. No other special instruments need to be learned to write a novel—no engine or body parts to memorize, no scalpels or brushes to hold for the first time. You may assume that if you can read and enjoy a good novel, you already know what goes into making one.

But in fact, the novel, and all forms of fiction, are as complexly assembled as any symphony or fine automobile. Creating one requires many subtle skills that must be practiced and acquired over time.

This was the most important lesson I learned from Leonard Bishop, though he didn't express it in quite those terms. It was the lesson that freed me to write. Leonard was brutally honest about the flaws in our work, but his belief in us was just as uncompromising. That belief was a veritable fountain to a crew of exceedingly thirsty writers, many of whom went on to publish novels.

By the way, the ones who went on to publish novels were not necessarily the most talented or witty or sensitive. They weren't necessarily the most compassionate or deserving. Some of them chewed gum loudly during the workshop.

But all of them were (or are) relentless, patient and tough.

That's what all novelists have to be. That was another lesson I learned from Leonard Bishop, and sometimes, when I'm down to typing about one letter a minute, I hear him nagging us to stop fooling around and write the damn things, and I miss him dreadfully.

PART ONE

Getting Started

CHAPTER ONE

You've Been Thinking Long Enough

The Gestation Period

Once upon a time, you got an idea for a novel.

Maybe when you broke up with your last boyfriend you vowed to write about your turbulent relationship, so the whole world would know what it was like to date the world's most annoying man, a man who wouldn't eat anything but Thai food.

Maybe when you were working on a construction site, you used to dream of writing about the beauty of a structure you had created with your own hands, and the fellowship that emerges among people laboring together.

Maybe on your vacation to Hawaii, you became fascinated with the myths of the island. You imagined a fantasy novel with Pele, Goddess of Fire, as your main character.

Maybe you've gotten a lot of ideas. Or maybe you haven't actually gotten anything that you would dignify with the name "idea," but you keep thinking that you'd *like* to get one.

Either way, you keep thinking about writing a novel. Isolated in traffic, when your favorite song comes on the car radio, you shiver, recognizing a fellow artist. You want to infuse your book with that same elusive, but powerful, emotion. *Someday, someday*, you promise yourself.

This thinking and dreaming time is the part of writing a novel that is entirely fun and risk-free. No one points out a cliché or tells you that the novel is a withering art form.

A novel requires this gestation period. (Writers often talk of their books as their "babies," and the metaphor holds in many respects, including how much we love them, and how much joy and grief they cause us.) During the gestation period, you keep your unborn book all to yourself. It grows inside you, while you wonder what it will be like when you write it.

This is also an important time creatively. Since you haven't started, there's not a lot of pressure. Ideas simmer in your subconscious, until the bubbles rise to tickle your nose. Your characters are ghostly, but charming, companions.

Once, shortly before I began work on a novel, I was taking the ferry from San Francisco to Sausalito, and the idea for a pivotal scene came to me. It was one of those rare, magical moments, and I thought, *hey, this is easy*. Alone on the deck, I wanted to take a bow, or even get down on my knees. Who knows where ideas come from, really?

The length of the gestation period varies. You may need a few months of "thinking" about a novel, maybe more. It all depends on you and the complexity of the idea you're going to tackle.

But if you are reading this book—even in a store—the odds are pretty darn high that you've been thinking long enough.

Procrastination—the Writer's Terminal Disease

"I'm thinking about a novel," is the first of many excuses that writers use to procrastinate. We believe that if we think about it long enough that when we sit down to write it, the words will flow easily.

You put it off until you graduate college, because then you won't be worried about keeping up your grades, and you'll have time. You tell yourself you have to "live it up before you put it down." Then you wait to find a job, so you can pay the bills. Then, all of a sudden there are a *lot* of bills to pay, and maybe even some more mouths to feed. Now you're waiting for your next promotion, for the kids to start school, for the den to get painted. You're waiting to become independently wealthy, to get a personal note of encouragement from John Updike, for someone to invent a really practical way to clean up the dust bunnies under the bed, to master vogue dancing.

You're waiting for a miracle.

Have I Got News for You

Yes, you need *down*time, dreaming time, a gestation period. But a longer gestation period does not translate into easier writing or a better book. Think about a book for *too* long and you'll start to lose interest in it, as the circumstances of your life and your perspective on your idea changes. (If you want to write about your high school sweetheart, and really make us believe she's the only sweetheart you'll ever have, you'd better do the writing before you have too many more sweethearts.)

You will never have enough leisure, confidence, money or support to write. Writing is time-consuming, angst-ridden and seldom pays well. There will never be an easy time to write, because writing is hard.

That's the bad news. Now, the good news: Since there will never be a better time, you might as well get that novel started— now.

"That" Novel and Whence It Comes; This Book and Whence It Came

What makes a novelist a novelist is not an unusual life but the desire to be a novelist. Put a novelist to work in a hardware store and he may get an idea for writing about a hardware store. Or he may fantasize about a science fiction novel, in which aliens land in toaster-shaped aircraft.

I've always wanted to write about anything that happened to me, including experiences that in retrospect seem pretty banal. Even back when I went to summer camp, I thought, "Hmmm, I'll have to write a novel about summer camp someday." I never did— that's what happens when you put an idea off for too long—but I still remember the crush I had on one of the camp directors, the tension of jockeying for a good seat at the dinner table, the comfort of the folk songs we sang to someone's guitar—and how I wanted to put all that into words.

When I started telling people I was a novelist, they often said to me, "I want to write a book someday."

Well, why not now? I would ask, and they would sputter, "someday" a few more times, or switch to "eventually," for a change of pace.

Probably most of them were not particularly driven to become authors, which is fine. If one is not driven to become an author, one should not become one, because there are a lot of authors already, and the world would be a hard place to live if there were no one left to drive buses or trade options.

But sometimes, at least, I sensed genuine frustration on the part of a person who really was willing to make the necessary sacrifices to write and publish a book, but who didn't know where to begin.

If my own writing had gone well that day (in other words, if I had successfully battled the urge to throw my computer out the window and jump out after it), I would launch into a frenzied diatribe about how they should get started. Some people appreciated that, and others backed away, as people often will when confronted with missionary zeal.

But all these encounters caused me to reflect on what it takes to get started — to bridge that Grand Canyon between thinking about, and actually writing, a novel.

Those reflections, once organized, became a seminar titled *Get That Novel Started!* that I give at a marvelous resource for writers called Writers Connection, in Cupertino, California. That seminar has become this book.

Do you have a "that" novel, nibbling or gnawing at you, demanding to be written? Have you dreamt of hearing a stranger sigh, "I loved your book"? You may not even be able to express exactly why you want to be a novelist, but if that *is* what you want, then your skin fairly tingles when you walk into a bookstore and see the new arrivals laid out in the rack.

I will tell you up front that writing and publishing a novel can be a long and difficult process that requires a deep commitment. But I also want you to know that it is definitely a realistic, attainable goal.

Or, as John Gardner put it, in *On Becoming a Novelist*: "Nothing is harder than becoming a true novelist, unless that is all one wants to be, in which case, although becoming a true novelist is hard, nothing else is harder."

You Can Get There From Here

Most of this book is about getting started. We'll talk about the challenge of finding time to write, and the barriers that might be in your way. We'll talk about where to look for ideas, and then we'll go step by step through a novel as it progresses from idea to outline to opening chapter.

Finally, we'll discuss ways to pace yourself, to keep alive your own interest in this long-term project, and where to go for more help.

In the introduction I pointed out that writing doesn't require special tools, like scalpels or mink brushes. What's unfortunate is that fact sometimes makes writers seem like fakers, because, sure, anyone can unplug the phone and turn on the TV and say, "Don't bother me. . . . My novel's gestating."

But what it also means is that you can assemble a novel with common household items. If you don't have a personal computer, you probably have a typewriter. If you don't have a typewriter, you probably have a pen and a pad of paper.

If not, go next door and borrow one.

TO GET THAT NOVEL STARTED

Realize that you are fully equipped. Make today the day.

CHAPTER TWO

A Journey of a Hundred Thousand Words Begins With One Sentence

The Balancing Act

To write a book, one must first find the time to write. Many of us juggle the competing demands of family, friends, jobs, dates, community work, home maintenance, hobbies, schoolwork—and we have the temerity to dream of an occasional day at the beach on top of that.

We'd have trouble writing an extra Christmas card—and we say we want to write *novels?*

You must make some changes. But you really don't have to quit your job, leave your family, and go live in the woods. In fact, I recommend against making immediate, drastic lifestyle changes, so you can stop worrying about whether or not your local monastery will accept your application.

Writing is a lot like exercising. If you wanted to run the Boston marathon (and a novel is definitely the marathon run of fiction writing), you wouldn't simply enter yourself, show up on race day, and expect your natural talent to take you to the finish. Rather, knowing that you set yourself an admirable and difficult goal, you would train: by eating right, and by running short distances, getting in shape to endure the twenty-six plus miles that the race requires.

So it would be asking a lot of yourself, on day one of your writing career, to sit down for four hours and churn out thirty pages, just as it would be asking a lot of yourself to bench press 300 pounds your first day in the gym.

Instead, you need to find ways to write a little bit each day, then gradually expand that time into a longer period that you can live with on a regular basis.

Recognize at the outset that writing a book is long-term project. It's probably not realistic to expect to knock off a salable novel in six months, unless you are both fairly experienced and sticking very close to the conventions of a particular genre (i.e., a romance novel or a western).

Realistic expectations are a good armor against the kind of disappointment that leads to discouragement. The novel will not be written in a few days, but it will be written.

Here's how.

The Ten-Minute Prescription

Start by writing ten minutes a day. That's right, just ten minutes a day. For the first few weeks, that's enough.

You say you don't have ten minutes a day? Su-u-ure you do.

You can get up ten minutes earlier and write before your day begins, or stay up ten minutes later and write when it's over.

If you work in an office, you can trim ten minutes from your lunch hour (maybe you were taking an hour and ten minutes anyway). You can stay at the office for an extra ten minutes and write at your desk (your boss will just think you're working extra hard). You can stop at the library for ten minutes on your way home. You can write on the commuter train or ferry.

If you are at home with children, postpone your errands and housework for ten minutes after they leave for school. Summer vacation? Be firm: Make a deal with the kids that you have a short time each day during which they are not to interrupt you. If that becomes the most likely time for them to fall off their bikes or set the cat's tail on fire, contract with your partner that he or she is responsible for them for even just a short time after dinner. You can do the same for him or her during another part of the day.

Yes, even the parent of preschool-age children can find a little time to write, if he or she can be exceedingly firm about afternoon naps, and not worry overmuch about the laundry.

If you are working eight hours a day behind a cosmetics counter at Macy's, and moonlighting as a bartender at night — rejoice! you probably have at least an hour between shifts.

I don't wish to minimize the demands on your time or to trivialize your financial responsibilities. I want to put a stop to any excuses. If you're going to make excuses, at least realize that that's what they are.

Even if finding ten minutes a day means that you have to write during a bumpy bus ride, you can probably tolerate the faint nausea for ten minutes. Hey, if you had to, you could hang by your thumbs for ten minutes a day.

If you are wondering how a novel can be written in ten-minute increments, you are right to wonder.

The important thing is to get started. My "ten minutes a day" prescription is meant to be a wedge, to get writing into your life, and to start collecting some pages. Once you make that first step and have a book under way, it becomes much easier to get up half an hour, or even an hour, earlier, or to stay up later, or to eat lunch at your desk instead of going to a restaurant.

One of the paradoxes of writing is that when your novel is going well, that your friends call less often, your job gets done faster and your partner develops a lovable habit of saying, "Don't worry, dear, I'll take care of it." You may find you do the same amount of house- and paperwork in less time than you did before, freeing up hours you didn't know existed.

If you can build up to an hour a day of writing, and use that hour faithfully, that will be enough. Many novels have been written in an hour a day. It requires discipline — a rarer, more valuable quality than talent — but it can be done.

Obviously, more is better. If you're able to work part-time, and/ or your children are grown or in school, or you happen to win the lottery, you are fortunate (although those situations, too, create possible problems, which we'll discuss later).

If not, that's still no excuse not to write.

What is absolutely crucial at this stage is that you do it every day — yes, seven days a week. Your mind, just like your body, has to be trained to perform certain tasks. If you wait until Saturday — "I'll have the whole afternoon!" — I can almost guarantee that will be the day that the pipes in the basement burst, or the dog mysteriously starts throwing up, or you do.

If nothing else, the big-screen television you've been wanting to buy for two years will go on sale (for one day only) and you'll *just have* to drive thirty miles to the warehouse to get it.

Daily work will stimulate your unconscious to keep simmering over the novel during nonwriting hours, so you are really making maximum use of your time. Continuity is very important in a novel; you need to be able to hold a lot of information in your head, so you need to remind yourself constantly of what you're doing. If you work regularly during the week, then you *will* be able to use a long block of time if it comes your way over the weekend or on a day off.

Same Time Tomorrow

Just waking up with the determination to get ten minutes of writing done "sometime" during the day isn't quite enough. A surprisingly large amount of writing is simply habit. Find the time that works best for you and stick to it. If your house catches fire during your allotted ten minutes, stay at your typewriter until the page in front of you turns to ash. Then you're allowed to get up for another sheet of paper.

You will be tempted to bargain with your sacrosanct time. ("I haven't seen Janine for so long, I must have lunch with her—I'll write when I get home." "I'm catching a cold, maybe I'll skip today.") Resist temptation. Get the habit. Open that notebook—even for ten minutes.

Other Stories

I heard about one writer so starved for privacy (he had a small apartment full of young children) that he would go out to his car for an hour in the evening and work under the dome light. While it didn't do the battery of his car a lot of good, he did manage to get some work done.

One much-published novelist told me how he got his start: He was working in telemarketing, selling magazine subscriptions. Between phone calls he would jot down a few sentences at a time on the index cards that were supposed to be used to keep records of the calls. Later, after work, he would sit in a coffee shop and expand upon this cryptic writing.

Legend has it that Jean Genet, the French novelist and playwright who started writing while in prison, began his first novel with a stolen pencil, writing on the brown paper that the prisoners were employed in using to make paper bags.

We can admire the heroism and determination of these people and still know that they were ordinary people who simply wanted to do something badly enough. What have you wanted to do badly? Learn to play the guitar? Save for a Camaro? Backpack through Europe? What you've wanted to do badly you have probably made the time, and found the resources, to do.

Set Priorities

Let's say you've set aside your ten minutes, and you're as regular as a metronome about using them. Every night you come home from work, scarf down a microwaved Lean Cuisine, then stay at the kitchen table to write. But most evenings you have a seven-ton report to read for the next day's sales conferences, so when your ten minutes are up, you must, with a sigh, tear yourself away.

Now you can start making some accommodations so that you can expand those ten minutes to an hour — or more — if possible. At this point, it will be easier, because you will feel your writing muscles grow stronger. You will see the evidence of your work unfold before you. You will have pages collecting in a box or notebook, and this will be something worth fighting for.

Once again, that doesn't mean that you have to go from ten minutes to ten hours a day overnight. Rather, take a look at your life and see how you can gradually phase out other commitments. If the novel is important to you, you will be willing to give some other things up.

Novelists tend to be hard workers and overachievers — who else would tackle a novel in the first place? But that may mean that you've also taken on a lot of other projects, all of which you do better than anyone else. You may feel that you are the only mom who can run the school bake sale, or the only dad who can coach Little League. You may indeed be the only one on your bowling team who can score over 100, or you may be the best volunteer at the crisis hotline.

Giving up some of these extracurricular activities will be difficult, and not just because *they* need *you*. If you are a good bowler or hotline volunteer, for example, you are getting regular feedback on your performance. You may not always score the highest on the team or offer adequate comfort to a caller, but you are able to measure your progress as you go, and to see the results of your actions, meanwhile enjoying the immediate gratification of being out with your friends or helping a worthy cause.

By contrast, the work you do on your novel may not have any impact on anyone for as long as several years. At the very least you are not going to get the same instant response to it. Sitting alone at your desk and coming up with a marvelously profound insight, no one applauds the way they would when you bowl your third consecutive strike. To choose to give up some evenings out to engage in solitary interaction with a piece of paper or a computer screen is a tough choice. Only you can decide whether you want to do it.

Other choices are tougher still. It's one thing to give up a hobby, your social life, or even a good cause. But what about the girlfriend you don't want to lose, the kids you don't want to neglect, and the boss who does some very important writing of her own: signing your paycheck?

Look at it this way: You only have to take one daily hour away from your work and love life (granted, that's pretty much the minimum you must take). It's one daily hour for yourself. That shouldn't ruin anyone's childhood or completely jeopardize your career or relationship.

Recognize that a novelist needs a streak of selfishness. Some of us have streaks as wide as the interstate, but if you are more the caretaker-to-the-world, can't-say-no-to-a-friend type, you may have to cultivate a little self-centeredness, at least when it comes to your book.

The Filler in Your Life

How much time do you spend watching television? Television is to writing as hemlock was to Socrates. I'm not just talking about "The Guiding Light" or reruns of "Cheers." Some people feel it's okay to have the boob tube blaring as long as PBS or the local news is on. But one newscast per day is plenty to keep you informed. After that you tend to get into human interest features about cuddly zoo animals anyway.

You don't have to dust the furniture twice a week or wash your car every Saturday afternoon. Maybe you don't need that monthly facial.

In *The Writing Life*, Annie Dillard describes how she let all her houseplants die while she was finishing a novel. Annie Dillard had dead plants, but she also has a Pulitzer Prize.

Take My Job—Please

If you are like the Lean Cuisine eater with the seven-ton sales report, the best thing you can do is look at how to "downsize" your job. Depending on what you do, perhaps you can take on fewer clients, patients or accounts, or become a freelancer or consultant. In some professions, and some locations, a consultant can make as much or more money in fewer hours.

Otherwise, you just might have to stay up an extra half-hour to read those sales reports. In that case, do the fiction writing when you are freshest. If you've read a lot of reports over the years, you probably know the drill on them by now, and they won't require as much concentration.

Some writers find that working three or four days a week, sometimes for longer hours, works better for them. The novelist Donna

Gillespie (*The Light Bearer*) told me, "Having three [consecutive] days off made all the difference. On those three days I would immerse myself in the book. . . . On days when I work eight hours I try to write for at least one or two hours a night."

If you have the choice to make, keep in mind that a job that does not require you to do much writing, or even much reading, has some definite advantages. If you're driving a cab, selling ice cream, waiting tables or building houses, you are moving your body and using a different part of your brain than you do as a novelist. During your off-hours, you will have more energy for fiction than the lawyer who writes appellate briefs, the public relations person who writes press releases, or the journalist who writes news stories.

Contact with people gives you an opportunity to observe them in their natural habitat, which in turn leads to more material. Why not get material as well as money from your job?

Just being physically active at work (or elsewhere) stimulates creative thought. Dorothea Brande, in her classic book *On Becoming a Writer*, describes how writers learn to enter "a state of light hypnosis," by pursuing any activity that is "rhythmical, monotonous, and wordless." When you are stuffing envelopes, bagging groceries or sticking widgets onto doohickeys as they pass by you on a conveyor belt,

> The attention is held, but *just* held; there is no serious demand on it. Far below the mind's surface, so deep that he is seldom aware . . . that any activity is going forward, [the writer's] story is being fused and welded into an integrated work.

Delegation, the Writer's Friend

One way of giving yourself more time to write is to pay someone else to do the things that are keeping you from writing. There are plenty of people who would love to earn money doing your gardening, housework, bookkeeping, childcare, even your personal errands. Obviously, this only makes sense up to the point that you can afford it. Don't engage a staff of servants on the theory that you'll recoup the investment on your first advance. That may indeed happen; but most first advances are relatively small, so it's not a very effective way to manage your finances in the meantime.

Otherwise, let the dust collect and the dishes pile up.

Too Much Time on Your Hands

If you are one of those who has to scrape writing hours together, you may be skeptical that it's possible to have *too* much time to write. *Au contraire, mon ami!*

Consider the case of Annabelle, a young woman who has recently inherited enough money to quit her job for a year and write that novel she's always wanted to write.

Annabelle worked for the past several years as a sales representative for a medical supply company. She used to arrive at the office at nine, make a series of phone calls to set up appointments, then hit the road to see customers. She checked in for messages, stopped for lunch, and hit the dry cleaners between sales calls. At five she stopped by her office again, then headed home for the evening.

This morning, on her first day of liberty, she awakens as usual at 7:30. She can spend the whole day on that novel!

What? The whole day?

On the road, in and out of offices all day, Annabelle longed for the solitude in which to create.

Be careful what you wish for.

Annabelle hides under the covers, trying to go back to sleep. Being chained to a typewriter until bedtime seems a Promethean fate, to put it kindly. When she didn't have time to write, Annabelle's ideas seemed to be bubbling just under the surface. Suddenly they have evaporated.

Obviously, the writer whose other obligations will not interfere with his or her writing is fortunate. A retired businessman; the writer whose spouse is able and willing to pay the rent; anyone without young children; someone blessed with an independent income; a person whose material needs are simple. Having the leisure to work is clearly the optimum situation for a budding novelist.

It also has its pitfalls, however. There's no boss to overhear your personal phone calls, and therefore to stop you from making them. There are no appointments to keep, except your appointment with a very inhospitable and stubborn typewriter. You work alone, without co-workers to snitch pencils off your desk and remind you that you are alive. The day is not easily divisible into particular tasks. Faced with long, intimidating hours, one easily becomes overwhelmed.

My advice to Annabelle and to those in similar (enviable) situations is *also* to start with ten minutes a day and build up gradually. The analogy to writing as physical exercise applies equally to all writers: No matter how much time you had to work out, you still wouldn't bench press those 300 pounds on your first day in the gym.

Once you've done your ten minutes, then go ahead and enjoy the rest of your day. Ten minutes isn't a lot, but it is ten minutes *spent writing*, ten minutes of honest effort, be it in front of ruled pad or computer. If all you do during those ten minutes is type the words to the "Star-Spangled Banner," you are entitled to feel that you have accomplished something, besides being a patriot.

It will take a few weeks, maybe even a month or more, to learn to become your own time manager. Meanwhile, experiment with some of these techniques:

1. Make two or three writing appointments for yourself, for example, at 9 A.M., 11 A.M. and 2 P.M. If you'd rather do it all at one stretch, then firmly commit to beginning at a certain time of day, be it eight in the morning or at 12:30 A.M., when all that's on TV are those half-hour commercials for baldness cures. (Some writers prefer the morning, others are at their most creative when everyone else is asleep.)

2. Schedule other events for the day. Not so many that you won't have time to write, but activities that will bracket your writing time and make those work sessions both manageable and harder to postpone.

For example, plan to swim or jog or even take a walk at some point during the day. Physical exercise will not only help structure your day but, as I noted earlier, it's marvelous for loosening ideas from where they lie plastered inside your head. (The novelist Rita Mae Brown, in *Starting From Scratch*, her writer's manual, exhorts, "Exercise will make you more productive. You've probably got a favorite sport. Do it.")

Meet someone for lunch, especially someone who must get back to work, so that your lunch date won't extend too late into your afternoon.

3. Reward yourself for a segment of writing time, or a certain number of pages, completed. "When I finish this section I can call my friend Sheila," or "I'll write until four, and then I get to watch 'Oprah.' " Treat yourself to something you enjoy. The more mindless and unconstructive the reward is, the better, but nonfood and nonsubstance rewards are preferable; that is, avoid the cookie and

the cocktail, especially if those are troublesome areas for you. If your credit cards pant with exhaustion when you remove them from your wallet, then you should also avoid shopping as a reward.

Sometimes, after a few tough hours pounding those keys, going grocery shopping will seem like a splendid outing to look forward to.

4. The at-home writer with all day to write might benefit more than others from going out to work at the library or a cafe. Going somewhere else simulates going to a job. Perhaps you will befriend a kindhearted librarian, waiter or waitress who will take an interest in your work, and ask you how it's going. Then, you have to show up; you can't let this good person down.

As weeks and months go by, you won't have to be so vigilant with yourself. As writing becomes a routine, distractions will lose some of their power.

Finally, don't isolate yourself too much. Certainly it's more common to find would-be writers in the situation described at the beginning of this chapter, in which the company softball team and keeping up with Grandpa's stamp collection eclipse all writing hours. But the other extreme isn't good, either. If you don't have contact with other people, if you don't have some activities and social events to anticipate—a reason to get dressed up and out of the house occasionally—then not only will it be difficult to write productively, but you will have less material to write about.

How Much Is Enough?

If you can write three hours a day, you are working as much as most full-time, published novelists do (though note that this means three hours, seven days a week). Once you've been writing for a while, taking Sundays or even weekends off is hardly fatal, but I must repeat how strongly I recommend that you write daily during the first year.

It's an extremely rare writer who can work more than five hours a day over any extended period of time. The most notable exceptions occur when a novelist is nearing the end of a project, and doing fine-tuning that doesn't require as much deep thought. Then he or she may be up for a weekend marathon.

If, however, you are one of those writers who can do five-plus hours at a stretch, then do so, and you have my admiration. I would never discourage anyone from time he or she wants to spend writing. But three to four hours a day is enough time to do some fairly serious work. Remember, I'm not only talking about three hours a day, seven days, *this week* — I'm talking about three hours a day, five to seven days a week, every week for a couple of years or more.

It adds up.

Doing Hard Time

As a novelist you must be prepared for a certain lack of understanding on the part of nonwriting humans. If you are a full-time writer, and you tell people that you work three or four hours, you will often be asked, "What do you do the rest of the day?" You might reply, with a dramatic roll of the eyes, "Recuperate from the draining creative process." Then pass your hand wearily over your forehead.

There would be some truth to that. When you talk about writing three hours, you're talking about some of the most concentrated work there is. At a regular job, chances are you spend a certain amount of time brewing coffee, phoning home or reading the paper, and calling it work.

Some of the rest of a full-time writer's day might be spent on research for the novel or reading the manuscripts of other people in her writing group. But if you spend three hours a day writing, and the rest of the day at the beach, you are a writer, and don't let anyone on this planet tell you otherwise.

TO GET THAT NOVEL STARTED

Set aside ten minutes to write, every single day.

CHAPTER THREE

Write What You Want, and the Novel Will Follow

Now What?

"All right," you say. "I've cut down my hours at work; I've bribed my partner to do the yard work; I've bought the kids enough Nintendo games to keep them in their rooms until they leave for college. What if I don't even know what my novel is about yet?"

No problem. As I've said, all you need is the desire to write. Let's assume you don't even have the seed of a germ of an idea. Later, we'll talk about how to find those seeds, and how to take them and plant them so that they grow into an actual living, blooming book, but let's assume for the moment that you don't even have a seed.

Just start writing about something. Leonard Bishop always said, "Writing begets writing," and he was correct.

So get yourself a journal, or a writer's notebook. This can be a $1.49 spiral from the five-and-dime or a needlepoint-covered blank book you bought at a craft fair. Or you can keep your journal on your computer, and print it out at the end of the day, or the end of the week, if you trust your computer.

Some people like the feel of an elegant fountain pen in their hands, while others are distracted by the ink blots. Some people like the rougher texture of fine vellum paper, while others feel guilty messing it up. Some people like to type because it's faster for them. Choose the method or methods that facilitate your writing.

Then *start*. Try these ideas:

1. *Write about something unusual you saw the day before.*

". . . The other day at the variety store the woman ahead of me was checking out with a package of Raisinets, a box of Velveeta cheese, a large bottle of mineral water and Tylenol. I tried to imagine what she was planning to do with this stuff. Was she filling requests from roommates who had headaches and sugar cravings?

Was she pregnant and getting an urge for Velveeta melted over Raisinets? . . ."

2. *Write about the first time you did something.*

". . . The bike felt so wobbly as I stood next to it I couldn't imagine how anyone could ever ride one. My older brother had been riding a bike for two years, but then he could do many things I couldn't, including talk to girls.

"My father promised to hold on to the back, but he had that looking-at-his-watch look, that half-time's-almost-over look, and I wasn't so sure that he wouldn't abandon me mid-block. . . ."

3. *Try to imagine how your parents met.*

". . . They were young then, younger than I am now. From the pictures I've seen, my father was unusually handsome, with a long, straight nose and curly black hair, and even the suggestion of a cleft chin.

"Still, I don't think my mother was too impressed that day he shouted at her from his Thunderbird, asking directions to the nearest gas station. . . ."

4. *Write about the worst date you ever had.*

". . . My aunt gave him my phone number without asking me if she could. What could I do when he called? I wasn't seeing anyone else; I didn't have an excuse. I guess I could have *pretended* to be seeing someone else, but Aunt Betty had pretty much told him everything about me, and I admit I was a tiny bit curious, too. Except that I knew that anyone Aunt Betty gave my number to would be the greatest dork of the twentieth century.

"I was right: the evening we were supposed to go to the movies, he called, ten minutes before he was supposed to arrive, to tell me that an old girlfriend had come into town unexpectedly. That was bad enough, but instead of just canceling our date, he asked me, 'What do you think I should do?' He wanted me to let him off the hook, salve his conscience. . . ."

5. *Write about something you love to do.*

". . . The first rush of water when I dive in the pool is so cold, I feel it chill even my lungs. But then I'm stroking hard against the water, blowing out bubbles and raising my head to suck in more air, and I feel alive, conscious of every muscle, my mind joined with my body. . . ."

6. *Describe the view from your window.*

7. *Write a letter to a friend.*

8. *Imagine what your life would be like if it were perfect.*

9. *Summarize the plot of your favorite novel or movie* (it doesn't matter whether you get it exactly right).

10. *Write the words to as many Broadway (or Beatles or Elvis or Talking Heads) songs as you can remember.* Yes, this counts, too. In fact:

11. *A writer with an eighteen-month-old son made a list of the ten or so words he could say and spent a playful half-hour trying to make a little poem using just those words.* If you don't have a child at this delightful stage, try the same exercise with the English translations of every word you can remember from high school French or Spanish.

Copy these "jump-starters" down and keep them near your typewriter, or set aside the first few pages of your notebook for the list so you won't waste precious time trying to remember what you were supposed to write about when you didn't have anything to write about.

You will have your own ideas for similar topics to pursue, so carry a small notebook or a stack of index cards in your purse, pocket or briefcase. Keep a pad by your bed. When you do get an idea, write it down, and later transfer it to your master list.

But if you get an idea and you forget to write it down, don't worry too much. You are a writer, and there are more ideas where that one came from.

Note: You may be ready to let loose on your novel right this moment. That's good; do it. In chapter six we will discuss the ways that you can start developing the characters and mapping out the plot of your novel. Just know that if you need or want to use some of the above exercises, now or later, that's okay, and they are here for you.

The Journal Pit

When I was in junior high, I kept a diary that I was very secretive about. My secretiveness made my sister very curious and she longed for a peek. Finally I exploded, "I don't know why you want to read this — all that's written in it is, 'I'm so fat, I'm so depressed,' about a million times over!"

I'm exaggerating, maybe just a little. However, after a while, it did become very easy, and not very cathartic, for me to continually repeat the same laments over and over. ("Why doesn't that guy in algebra like me? Why do my thighs look like white Jell-O?")

So beware of using the journal to obsess about your life. By obsessing I mean repeating abstract concerns, asking questions with no answers. A journal can be helpful as an introspective tool, especially when combined with therapy, but that's not what we're doing here.

Rather, use the journal to begin to acquire a novelist's skills of observation. Identify specific objects, numbers and colors in the outside world. Describe how people look, or how they move. Create dialogues, even if from memory. Experiment. Stretch. Be stupid. No one ever has to see what you've written but you. Just keep it hidden from your sister.

Beware the Saboteur

Novelists are always insecure about their work, no matter how much they have published. Just try talking to an author after he or she reads a bad review of her latest novel. But you are at your most vulnerable when you are starting out.

About a year after I started writing I was at a party that was attended by a number of other writers, some of them published. I timidly told a woman novelist (who, I don't think, had even bothered to cut her Scotch with water) that I was at work on a novel. "What's it about?" she slurred. I briefly told her.

The woman staggered backwards a little, then caterwauled, "It sounds dumb!"

Looking back, I realize this good lady was too inebriated to know *War and Peace* from a dinner menu, but because she was published (and I didn't realize yet that published novelists were ordinary people!), I was deeply shaken, and even convinced, for a few days, that her judgment was correct.

Most writers like to encourage beginners, but a few feel the need to lessen the competition. And even more commonly, non-writing acquaintances will make discouraging remarks without meaning them. They just don't understand that wrinkling their noses or telling you about a novel with a similar story line will seem like a deathblow to your entire writing career.

So be choosy about whom you discuss your material with, especially at this early stage. If you tell someone that you are writing a novel and they want to know what it's about, explain politely that you don't discuss works-in-progress. (Most people have heard that one.) If it feels more comfortable, you can always give a brief, vague answer like, "Oh, it's this romance thing." Leave it at that. If you start a long summary of the plot, there's a good chance that the person's attention will wander off in the middle, or he will suddenly spot an old friend across the room. You've gained nothing except another reason to doubt yourself.

There's another, equally important reason for practicing this restraint: You should take the excitement you feel about your work to the work itself. If you casually discuss what you plan to write about, you lessen some of your drive to do the actual writing.

Similarly, don't repeat all the funny (or lyrical or insightful) lines you came up with that day to your friends. If they laugh, you will have a little less motivation to go back and make those lines even funnier, because you've already received some satisfaction from writing them. If they don't laugh, you will simply have more self-doubt fodder.

You *do* want to get feedback on your work-in-progress. For that, though, you will be going to your writing group or to a few trusted folks who you have cultivated as critics.

Your Personal Fan Club

You can dismiss a busybody at a party, but you certainly need to elicit support from family and friends. You may already be blessed with people close to you who fully support your literary ambitions. If that is the case, I hope you show them how very much you appreciate them, every single day of your life. These significant others who encourage you—who tolerate your absences and introspective moods—are doing so primarily on faith, because anyone who doesn't write fiction will have little understanding of the rigors and risks of the craft.

That being the case, don't feel bad if your loved ones exhibit, at first, some resistance to the idea of this grand new project you've taken on. They may give voice to all the common misconceptions: "But you've never written before!" "Isn't it impossible to get published?"

Remember that the best way to get others to take you seriously is to take yourself seriously. You don't have to be huffy about it, just honest: "I've always wanted to do this, and now I am."

As time goes by, and you continue to work, people around you will accept that this is something you do. As you set priorities, and cut down on your television watching and club hopping, you will be sending a signal to them that writing is worth some sacrifices to you.

You'll be nice, of course. You will be aware that you are asking people to spend less time with you, people for whom that is a loss. You may be doing less gourmet cooking for them, or coming home from work an hour later. You'll look for ways to make it up to them. (At the very least, consider a novel dedication!)

Even as your friends come to think of you as a novelist, they may call you at home, thinking, "Well, she's only writing," and they may feel rejected when you cut the conversation short. Don't be too hard on them—someone who doesn't write fiction will not know how difficult it is to reestablish one's delicate concentration after an interruption—but cut the conversation short anyway.

Or, avoid the above problem entirely by getting an answering machine (they're not very expensive, if you don't already have one). Screen your incoming calls. True, you may get an occasional message along the lines of, "I know you're there—you're writing, aren't you?" but consider that a compliment. Meanwhile, it's much easier to call someone back later than to disengage oneself prematurely.

A Place for You

Virginia Woolf is well known for saying that one must have a room of one's own in order to write.

If I ruled the world I would make corner suites in modern high rises available to every novelist. I would provide a receptionist and free coffee, and there would be views of bucolic fields or constellations of city lights, whichever the writer found more inspiring.

Until I am elected to rule the world, however, we will have to make some compromises.

You may have the resources to rent yourself an office, which is fine. But it is not crucial to have a private office with the latest in word processing technology to be able to write. That can easily become another excuse to postpone writing. People say, well, "I have to go out and rent a space with *ambiance*," or "I have to wait 'til Johnny goes to Yale so I can use his room," or "I have to save up for that AKZ 989 voice-activated laser jet combination modem and coffeemaker."

Watch out for anything that lets you postpone writing.

Still, creating some separate space for yourself does make writing easier, especially as you begin to collect notes, chapters and completed drafts. See what you can carve out of your existing quarters. If you have an extra room, go stake it out now—quick, before your mother catches on to what you're doing and decides to move in, or your boyfriend gets a sudden yen to install a pool table.

If you live alone it won't be hard. There's always the dining room table—in modern America, probably more dining room tables are used as desks than for entertaining anyway. Even if you just have a studio apartment, you can use the coffee table that goes with your fold-out couch.

For many years, I wrote in the living room of my one-bedroom apartment, which was possible first because I lived alone, and later because I had married a workaholic who believes that long-term mind-breaking projects build character. People who came over had the pleasure of gazing at scattered papers piled as high as snow-drifts. On the rare occasions that I entertained, I took the trouble to consolidate these papers into fewer, but higher, drifts.

More suggestions:

> "Fold-out" desks can be put in a living room or bedroom and folded up at the end of the day, or whenever you want to hide your work-in-progress from guests.
>
> You can divide a room with a folding screen.
>
> If you have a garage, write there and park in the driveway for now. Your paint job won't last as long, but you're still one step ahead of the writer who worked under his dome light.
>
> A walk-in closet can become an office. So can a sun or laundry room. Or make sure the burners are off, and put a nice, smooth piece of wood on top of the stove, and write there.
>
> Remove the fatal distractions. If possible, don't write in a room with a television or refrigerator. Put the phone out of reach.

But you don't have to model your writing space after the solitary confinement cells in Alcatraz, either. It's okay to have a few little battery-chargers around — a newspaper or some recorded music. As you work you'll learn what keeps you going but won't derail you.

If you prefer to write on buses, in cafes or at work, your corner at home can simply become the place where you keep your material as it accumulates. This is also where you can put your books about writing, your dictionary and your thesaurus. You can put a bulletin board up on the wall, where you tack up inspirational sayings, favorite snapshots or reminders to yourself ("Mention Celia's age somewhere in the first chapter").

It's good to be flexible about where you write, so that if you travel a lot or have to be away from home for any reason, you can adapt. But it's worth investing some time and energy in personalizing a writing area, in no small part because it reinforces the message you want to send to yourself and others: *I am a writer. This is important to me.*

No matter how humble or small your space, you can look with pride at your orange crate desk and the peeling paint on the walls and the spider on the ceiling who seems to smile when you come in.

Because now you know that you are not a would-be, someday writer. You are a today, now, present-time writer.

TO GET THAT NOVEL STARTED

Use your writing time. If you don't want to work on your novel, write something — anything — else.

CHAPTER FOUR

Breaking Through the Barriers

The Great Wall of Writing

Red Smith said that "writing is simple—you just open a vein." This is wise, yet deceptive. If writing were that easy, all you would need is a sharp knife.

For some, setting aside writing time and keeping a list of things to write about is like taking aspirin for a gangrenous leg: It may alleviate the pain, but it doesn't begin to address the real problem.

Our desire to write is strong and passionate, yet the barriers are equally formidable. Why? Writing is a risky business. As discussed in previous chapters, it's something that others around us don't always understand very well.

But even if you are from a family of writers, you are not necessarily in a more enviable position. I knew a man, James, who was the first cousin of a very well-known author about ten years older than he. James wanted to write very badly, but he believed (not without justification) that he would always be compared to his older cousin who already counted two *New York Times* best-sellers to his credit.

Because You Care

If writing is important to you, it will also be scary. You won't feel about it the way you might about some hobby you take up casually.

As a teenager, I occasionally went ice skating. I could get around the rink, and that was about all, but that was enough. I went to be with my friends, drink Cokes at the refreshment stand, and maybe even get a little exercise. It didn't bother me that I wasn't destined to be a championship skater. It didn't bother me (very much) when Collette O'Leary showed off her figure eights.

But the possibility that *I don't have it* as a writer threatens my identity. This, for years, has been who I am and who I want to be. Ironically, that means I can't always enjoy it as much as I would if it were just a hobby; I take every intimation of failure very hard.

The first time my younger sister and I went to the ice rink we laughed a lot, pointing to each other's buckling ankles and the wet spots we started to accumulate on the cuffs of our corduroy pants.

But when I started writing, I had wanted to do it for so long that I was terrified. I had to contemplate what would happen if I didn't "make it." How could I ever find something else I wanted to do as badly?

Writers may keep journals to chart their own inner experiences. They may play around with poetry or short humor pieces that they can enjoy sharing with their friends.

But no one writes a novel just "for fun." It's too big a job. Writing a novel for fun would be a little like building a house that you knew no one would ever live in, or even see. It would be like spending an entire weekend preparing a banquet for twelve, all the while planning to take one bite of the *coq au vin* and stuff the rest, and all the other courses, into the garbage disposal—but worse, because novels take longer than a weekend to write.

Voices of Doom

So it's understandable that fear is part of the writing package.

And there are many, many voices inside all of us who are eager to articulate those fears for us. Some are the internalized voices of parents, teachers and other adults who influenced us as children, when our egos were being pummeled into shape. Do any of these sound familiar?

> "No one can write like the great masters anymore." (Seventh-grade English teacher)
>
> "That's not a poem. It's only a limerick." (Fifth-grade teacher)
>
> "You don't have enough education to write a novel." (Thanks, Dad!)
>
> "You want to be a writer when you grow up? Now isn't that cute! Hey, Fran, little Bobby is going to write books— hahaha!" (Uncle Walter)

If you run out of the voices of authority figures from your past, you will probably be able to pick up where they left off. You may say to yourself:

> "I'll tell all my friends that I'm going to write a novel, and then I won't."

"Even if I write the novel and send it out, no one will publish it."

"Even if I publish the novel, I'll get bad reviews. They'll say my prose is banal and my characters are one dimensional."

". . . Then my ex-wife will recognize herself in it and sue me for everything I've got."

My friend James always imagined the voices of his acquaintances asking him, "Has your famous cousin read it yet?" James figured that he could only lose. If he failed as a novelist, people would *really* think he was a failure, because they thought he had such high-powered contacts in the literary world. If he succeeded, people would assume that his cousin had gotten him published. (By the way, it's certainly an advantage to know people in the publishing field, but that is no guarantee you will be published. Publishers are not going to bring out a book that they don't believe in; too much money and their too-valuable reputations are at stake. So if they do publish you, it's because you deserve it.)

What You Lose

Beginning to write definitely means you will lose something: the fantasies you had about writing. You may discover that it is a more difficult, slower process than you expected. Early success creates challenges, too (though we should all be so challenged): The writer who publishes his or her first story on the first try may not be prepared for the period of learning and the inevitable rejections still ahead.

Then, too, it is not only difficult to separate people's reactions to what you write from their reactions to you, it is tempting to take those reactions even more seriously. In a social situation you can be artificial, or at least keep your interactions on a surface level. If someone you meet at a dinner party doesn't seem immediately in awe of your sensitivity and intelligence, so what? All you talked about were recent movies and the food. You didn't expose your soul to this person. Who are they to judge you?

But in your writing, if it's any good at all, you will reveal intimate parts of yourself, whether you're writing an autobiographical novel about your divorce or a fantasy set in the land of Yrwalla. Others who read your work will know something about your values, your aspirations, your hurts. If the writing is "rejected," you may feel that those same feelings have been stomped on.

Here's the good news: If you aren't at least a little bit scared, you probably aren't prepared for what's in store. If writing isn't important enough to you to involve some risk, you may not want to do it all that badly.

That doesn't mean you have to let the fear stop you.

The Seven Demons

Here are seven categories that our fears tend to fall into. Although any kind of list will be an oversimplification of a process that is largely unconscious, a list is helpful because it is a way to name, and thus to gain control over, some of these internal forces:

Fear of Failure

The most obvious one. You will work for years and no one will care about anything you do. Your best shot won't be good enough. You will be embarrassed in front of family and friends for many generations to come.

Fear of Rejection

This is a prominent aspect of the fear of failure. As discussed above, fiction demands a healthy dose of self-exposure, so if an editor turns the book down, it's hard not to feel he or she has turned *you* down. You can keep your writing secret, or semi-secret. But even in the privacy of your mailbox, rejections will hurt.

Fear of Success

Some people are skeptical about this one, and indeed, the fear of success is a subtler concept than the fear of failure or rejection, though certainly familiar to psychologists. To succeed in a new endeavor means breaking with your past. Even if you have been successful in other areas, those, in fact, may be areas in which you have "permission" to be successful. Let's say that when you were growing up, your mother was an excellent homemaker, and your father a respected entrepreneur. Perhaps you have combined the two to become a good cook with a profit-turning catering business. Even so, you may carry lingering ambivalence about "artists," if they were looked upon by your family, as they are by some, as being lazy troublemakers who are given to substance abuse, sexual promiscuity or just plain weirdness.

These biases are the other side of society's fascination with artists: our glorification of them as divinely inspired, lovably eccentric and above the rules of normal behavior.

Then, too, if you gain recognition as a writer, your friends may envy you—and how much do you like the people you envy? You may fear that these same, so-called friends will secretly hope that you'll turn out to be a "one-book author," and that your success will conveniently vanish as quickly as it came.

All these possibilities make the status quo seem very appealing.

The Fear of Having Nothing to Say

Mustn't a novel shock people with the weight of its originality and the pure power of its insights?

The fear of having nothing to say may cause you to discard all your ideas immediately, deciding, *it's been done before*. This is an evil, deep-rooted form of writer's block: You are actually dismissing the idea of being a writer before you give yourself a chance.

Fear of Giving Offense or Arousing Controversy

The other side of the fear of having nothing to say is the fear of having *too* much to say. Suppose a character in your novel makes an unkind remark about senior citizens. *You* have nothing against senior citizens, but your character is a clod. Still, you can picture the elderly woman who will poke her cane into your chest when she sees you in the produce section of your local supermarket. "You mean man," she will say. "I want you to know you hurt my feelings dreadfully."

Your conservative friends will hate you when you expose your liberal sympathies (or vice versa). Your mother will have a massive coronary when she reads that sex scene.

Joking aside, you may indeed have controversy to raise, for example, if you're a teacher who wants to expose the flaws in the school system, or a doctor who wants to write about unnecessary surgeries that are performed.

Fear That Others Will Recognize Themselves

Every novelist draws, to a greater or lesser extent, from his or her own life. This doesn't mean that you're not creative. Believe me, there will be more than enough demands on your creativity, no matter how much you cannibalize your own life. No, writing about yourself and people you know isn't cheating. It's "using your material."

In the privacy of your room, you can write vividly and with great glee about all your best friend's annoying habits. But, you worry, when the book is published, are you going to be able to buy up every local bookstores' copies before she sees it? Is writing worth more than friendship? And aren't you going to be kind of lonely cashing your royalty checks and then going out to Christmas dinner alone, since no one is speaking to you?

Inertia

It's a law of physics. You're in a routine. You've been thinking about writing, rather than doing it, for a long time, maybe for years. Why not just keep thinking? It's easy to put off the novel for another month—two months, a decade—since you've put it off this long.

Mountains are built of sand, accumulating over millennia. Once the mountain gets there, it's hard to move. To write, you have to push your life out of the way, which takes more energy than it took to get it *in* the way when you weren't paying attention.

Inertia isn't a fear, exactly, but it's the most effective way fear has of stopping us. The mountain that is our life—our mortgage, our family, our Sunday dinners with the folks—looms even larger than it is, and the fears hide behind the mountain.

Have I scared you? No—you'd probably thought of all this and more already. (Whenever I doubt my own imagination, I remind myself of all the things I invent to worry about.)

All, some or none of the above may be holding you back. So let's deal with them now.

Some Logical Responses

We can begin, at least, by being logical.

The Fear of Failure

Obviously, you'll never know unless you try. You have a choice between risking the discovery that you are not cut out to be a writer, versus spending the rest of your life wondering if you could have done it if you'd had the nerve.

Besides, you don't need to take out an ad in your local paper, announcing that you are now a novelist. Sure, there is also a time to claim your ambitions proudly (and if your partner hears you clicking away at the typewriter in the middle of the night you probably won't get away with a story about dashing off a note to the milkman, especially since most people don't *have* milkmen anymore). When you're starting out, you don't have to tell everyone about your plans, either—it may make you feel more comfortable early on if you don't put yourself in the position of having a lot of people ask you, "So how's your book going?" every time they see you.

Of course, whoever you tell or don't tell, the person who cares the most about whether you write a novel is you, and, if you fail, you will have to deal with you. But if you don't try, you will have to deal with you. For what it's worth, the more you want to be a writer, the more likely you are to succeed.

The Fear of Rejection

As a writer, you have a distinct advantage in that you usually get your rejections by mail; although, ironically, that changes a little after you become more successful and editors know you personally—well enough to call and tell you that they didn't like something you wrote.

By mail or in person, rejections hurt. What you should remember, though, is that agents may not want to represent a novel because: 1.) they simply are not accepting any more clients, no matter how intriguing the author's work; 2.) they are unfamiliar with the marketing demands of your particular genre—i.e., mystery, romance or science fiction; 3.) they don't handle fiction at all (whether or not they handle fiction, nonfiction is usually what pays the bills); or 4.) they have some personal problems with the material—i.e., the subject of alcoholism arouses painful memories.

Editors may reject your book because: 1.) they simply aren't able to take another project; 2.) they already have a similar book on their list (this won't discourage another editor; novels are so unique that they don't compete with each other in the conventional sense); or 3.) just like an agent, they may have a personal negative response that has nothing to do with the quality of your work.

Agents or editors may or may not be honest about their personal reasons for turning a book down. Sometimes their criticism is vague and none too helpful: "A certain *oomph* is missing"; "The characters don't truly breathe." (Sometimes you want to scream: "Of course they don't truly breathe, you stupid editor—they're fictional!" Other times you just want to whine, "Okay, so you don't like the book. How about a six-figure advance anyway?")

Agents or editors may also reject your book simply because it needs another draft. So? Do another draft.

There are many occasions when a professional will take some serious time to try to pinpoint for you what doesn't work. In those cases, be open to what he or she has to say, especially if you get several rejections with similar complaints or advice. But don't rely entirely on rejection-letter critiques as the basis of your rewrites, and, if what editors tell you doesn't make sense, ignore it.

Remember that very famous novelists get rejected all the time. Oh, yes! Their editors make them do rewrites; paperback houses and new publishers may pass on their work entirely.

Also, keep in mind that there are "levels" of rejections. Anything but a preprinted rejection letter is encouragement to submit again. Often an editor will write, "I'd like to look at your next novel." At that moment, admittedly, writing another novel feels like getting to the moon on half a gallon of gas. But you will get there, so file away the editor's name and address. Look at it this way: Maybe the editor who buys your first novel won't offer you enough money for the second, so you can shop it around to all the editors who rejected your first but wanted to see your second.

Sometimes an editor will volunteer to read a later version of the same book he is turning down. Take him up on it and submit another draft (one that has more than minor changes).

Remember that it is always your writing, not you, that is being rejected. Your writing is always growing and improving (which is more than we can say for some people we know). With each rejection you are one letter or phone call closer to acceptance.

The Fear of Success

Selling your first book is a dramatic event. Here you've been working on this manuscript for months or years, and that's all it is—a manuscript. Then you get a phone call and all of a sudden you're a published novelist—now you have a *book*.

Life is perfect. You'll never doubt yourself again.

But, of course, you will. You know that your fundamental conflicts aren't so easily solved. Even after you get a really sharp book jacket and a pile of gushy reviews, you will have to confront anew all the things you don't like about yourself and the world. Life is hard. Your ears are still too big, and you could get called for jury duty anytime.

This is why, after a period of euphoria, people sometimes feel depressed when they get good news.

But what happens then is that you shift gears. You set the next goal for yourself—the second book, the biggest advance. The ambition you have, the ambition it takes to write a novel, will not be quenched by your first publication, believe me.

Your friends and family will have to adjust to your success, too; they will have to reclassify you, in their own minds, from struggling wannabe to published author.

Any change is difficult—but you will have rewards that more

than compensate. If you are moderately humble about your achievements, your old friends will admire and respect you more. Meanwhile, you will be entering a new circle of colleagues. And, while there are few things I can guarantee, one of them is that no matter how successful you are your writing will always challenge you.

The Fear That You Have Nothing to Say

There are no truly new ideas — *everything* has been done to death. How many young-men-coming-of-age novels are there? How many books about mothers and daughters are there, or murder mysteries?

In the movie industry, and even more so in television, "concepts" rule. This spawns frequent imitations of success, while less successful concepts preempt the field for similar ideas. If there was a popular series on last year with a flying disc jockey, that may make another producer very eager to jump in with a series about a weatherman who uses his psychic abilities to fight crime. Two years later, the craze for broadcast journalists with supernormal abilities may be deemed to have passed.

This phenomenon occurs in fiction, too. In the mid-seventies, Robin Cook published a gripping novel called *Coma*, which was deservedly a best-seller. As a story about a conspiracy at a Boston hospital to put people into comas to steal and sell their organs to wealthy transplant recipients, it was not only suspenseful and fast-paced, but it predicted some of the thorny ethical questions with which the medical community still grapples.

It was also the harbinger of a number of knockoff medical thrillers, books about evil doctors holding clearance sales on body parts at creepy hospitals (with titles like *This Won't Hurt a Bit* and *Ouch — Oh, Yes It Does*).

You can't guarantee your own success by writing a book like last year's best-seller because by the time you submit it for publication, it's likely that many other writers will have ripped off the same best-seller. Without more, yours will be just a cynical attempt at stealing another's glory.

So if you have an idea that you don't think anyone's ever had before, that is all to the good. Be like Robin Cook and invent yourself a genre. But remember that someone could have just as easily said to him, "Hey, Robin, what's so different about your novel? It's like half the stories Edgar Allan Poe wrote, just with high-tech anesthesia added."

I had two students in one class writing novels about their experiences as Peace Corps volunteers in Nigeria. The two books were so completely different that they not only didn't compete with each other, they made all of us more interested in both of them. We all became insatiable Peace-Corps-in-Nigeria groupies.

So if someone else publishes a book that you think is similar to your own, don't worry. It may create a market for the setting or events of your novel, which you will execute even more dramatically.

It is also true that, in fiction, no ideas are inherently good or bad. For the most part the type of novel you are writing or its setting is far less important than your execution of the novel. Television needs "high concept," but the writing doesn't go much further than that. Television doesn't rely on the writer's skillful use of language, and the morals and insights are usually delivered with all the subtlety of jackhammers.

Consider the concepts behind these novels:

- A has-been fisherman catches a marlin, but sharks eat it.
- A woman commits adultery a couple of times and then poisons herself.
- A man stirs up trouble on a mental ward and is lobotomized by the evil head nurse.

Boring, sexist, depressing ideas? They're also summaries of *The Old Man and the Sea*, *Madame Bovary* and *One Flew Over the Cuckoo's Nest*.

Just as your life is comprised of unique experiences—no matter whether they are extraordinary or commonplace—so will your translation of your ideas and your experiences to the page be unique. If you have the desire to write, it's *because* you have something to say, granted that you may have to perfect your skills of saying those things in the most compelling way.

This is the long way of telling you that the only way to find out whether you have something to say is to start wrestling words onto a page.

The Fear of Giving Offense or Arousing Controversy

Some of the very best books in the world aroused controversy or were even banned for periods of time. To name a few: Dalton Trumbo's *Johnny Got His Gun*, D.H. Lawrence's *Lady Chatterley's Lover*, Nabakov's *Lolita*, and James Joyce's *Ulysses*.

That doesn't mean you want to be gratuitously offensive just to get attention. (Authors have indeed often gotten attention for it, but that doesn't mean that people took their work seriously in the long run.)

Instead, if you are honest and true to your vision, your controversial work may even be able to change the world. John Steinbeck, in *The Grapes of Wrath*, and Upton Sinclair, in *The Jungle*, raised public awareness of serious social problems.

But when you're finished changing the world, what do you do about the old lady in the produce section who objects to your remark about the elderly? Explain that it was your character talking, not you. Explain that if she read your book the way you intended it she would understand that you meant the opposite of what she thought you meant. Then remind her about the First Amendment.

There's always another option, as well. If you have genuine reason for concern that what you have to say could threaten your livelihood, or seriously embarrass your loved ones, you can publish under a pseudonym.

The Fear That Others Will Recognize Themselves
You may be surprised, first, to discover how slow people are to locate themselves in your writing. If they do recognize themselves, or parts of themselves, they will more often than not be flattered to find that you have considered them interesting enough to fictionalize, even if you do include some of their less-than-noble traits.

But perhaps you want to write about an actual person who really is mean and nasty, the kind of person who'd kick a panhandler's cup just to hear the jingle. Well, it probably *won't* surprise you to hear that people are especially slow to recognize their own meanness; nevertheless, in chapter five we will address this problem more fully. There are ways of disguising characters that buffer everyone's feelings while giving you lots of leeway to draw from life.

For now let me emphasize as well that fictional characters almost always turn out to be combinations of many different real people with a lot of your own imagination thrown in. No matter how closely you start out writing about a real person, the character begins to grow on her own. Your story will also demand that she do things the real person has never had to do.

Inertia
Chip away at that mountain, a little bit at a time. Don't try to move the whole darned thing out of the way this afternoon.

Sit down today for ten minutes. That's the best advice I can give any aspiring writer, any time. This sets up momentum in opposition to the inertia.

Reality Calling

Unfortunately, "dealing logically with one's fears" is somewhat a contradiction in terms. The limits we set on ourselves are far more complicated, and far more tenacious. It's not like being lost on the Santa Monica freeway, where all you need is to pull over to a gas station and have someone point you in the right direction. Because the saddest truth of all is that there is a big part of us that wishes to remain lost.

Keep the logical arguments in mind anyway. Over time they will make more sense. Meanwhile, here are some exercises you can do to start breaking through the emotional barriers.

The Beast

First, identify the voice or voices whispering your fears to you. (See "Voices of Doom" earlier in this chapter.)

Let's say, as an example, that when you attempt to write you often feel uncomfortable because you're doing something that seems — well, frivolous. You keep saying to yourself that a man (or woman) your age, be that 15, 22, 35, 67 or 112, needs to be doing something *serious* with his or her life, not writing novels.

Let's further say that, on reflection, you can identify that voice as sounding suspiciously like your father's, who firmly believed in nine-to-five jobs, pension plans and nonassumable, fixed-rate home loans. (Why, your father would ask, would you ever need an assumable mortgage when you are never going to sell your house or move from that street or change jobs?)

You are convinced that your father, even though he lives several thousand miles away, hasn't spoken to you since Christmas of 1984, and has no idea that you have started a novel, would never approve of your plans to write. *What will your boss think?* you imagine your father would ask you. *Won't this interfere with your chance for that 7½-cents-an-hour raise?*

Don't call your dad and try to convince him that he's wrong about writing novels. Sure, he'll probably be thrilled to hear from you, and you may very well discover that he's mellowed incredibly since 1984. He may tell you that now that he's getting on he regrets the rigidity of his own youth. He wishes that he spent a few years in the merchant marines instead of seeing the world from the deck of a cruise ship in his retirement. "Go ahead and follow your dream, son (daughter)," he'll say. "Get that novel started!"

This will be gratifying, but unfortunately, it's too late for Dad's change of heart to have much impact. You're all grown up, and you've only been stopping yourself, with messages you internalized long ago. This voice within you, which may have been inspired by your father's values and behavior, is now a part of you. God bless Mom and Dad—they hit hard, with surgical strikes, and move on.

So listen again to the voice, which is part of you, and further personify it.

What does the voice sound like? Maybe it sounds—my, what a coincidence!—just like your father. But maybe it's snappish, like your third-grade teacher making fun of your penmanship. Or even sweet and soothing, like a beautiful woman assuring you, "Don't bother with that writing now. It's a waste of time, anyway."

Give "the voice" a name. It might be a given name that you've always hated—Herman? Gertrude?—or it might be something more like a title: The Big, Mean Ugly Guy, or even The One Who Stops Me. Be creative. Be silly.

Let's decide, for purposes of this exercise, that the voice is male, and name him Poindexter. Now, if Poindexter had a face, what would that face look like? Devilishly handsome? Disfigured? Like a Teenage Mutant Ninja Turtle or Tom Cruise? Maybe he has Cyrano's nose, Hitler's mustache or Dumbo's ears. Describe his face in a paragraph.

What about his body? Maybe Poindexter is a kind of monster—with purple octopus-like tentacles, or green reptilian skin. Since we know he's strong, maybe he bears a striking resemblance to Arnold Schwarzenegger. But he could just as easily look like the 98-pound weakling from the comic book ads for body-building schools. Describe the space he carves out of your imagination.

Remember that these are all just examples. Your voice might evolve into something male, female, human, animal or machine. But let's take everyone's voice-become-creature and call him, her or it, the Beast, although this Beast may have a seductive appearance, to better convince you not to write.

Now, go back to the original thoughts that led you to this Beast; the criticism that it offered to stop you from writing. Use that as the opening line of a dialogue with your new creation, Poindexter. Let him express his most virulent, damaging criticism, but fight back. Fight back and win.

Here's an example. Let's say you're a thirty-five-year-old man who works for an ad agency full-time, and who wants to write a novel in your off-hours. But your voice—"Poindexter," from above—is constantly hissing at you, "A man your age should be doing something serious with his life!"

Okay, that's the beginning of your dialogue. Now it's your turn. Write:

"I *am* doing something serious with my life. I work from nine to five and I make good money. And now I'm going to do something even *more* serious—I'm going to write fiction."

"Haven't you learned anything? If you ever want to become a partner, you're going to have to work a lot longer than nine to five, you lazy slob!"

"I'm doing fine at the agency, and I want to write a novel. What's the point of being a partner if I don't do the thing I really love?"

"You're too old to start something new."

"That's why I'm going to start now. I'm not going to get younger, and I'm not going to wait any longer."

"Give it up!"

"No! I won't! I've been listening to you all my life! I'm not going to let you stop me anymore!"

If you like, you can also expand this dialogue into a scene. That is, describe where you and Poindexter are and what you are doing. Experiment and take your time.

Below is an example of such a scene. It's written in the present tense; you can do that, too, or use the past tense. You can, in fact, do it any way you want. It can be two paragraphs or twenty pages.

Poindexter is picking up my stapler in his claws. He has an arm—I guess you could call it that—coming out of his forehead. The skin of this arm has spikes jutting out of it, thick and frightening as a porcupine's quills.

"What are you going to use this for?" he sneers at me. "You're not ever going to write more than one page, you'll never need a stapler!"

"You're a pain in the rear," I tell him. I am jiggling a large stone in my hand, a shiny rock I picked up in the woods one day and use as a paperweight. I want him to know I'll use it if I have to.

"I'm just here to tell you the truth, friend," he says. With his forehead-arm, he throws the stapler in the wastebasket and then sweeps some papers from my desk.

"Hey!" Now I'm really angry. I get up. Poindexter glares at me with all twelve of his bulging puke-green eyes. "Listen," I say, "I've got a novel to write. I'm giving you one more chance to get out of here and leave me alone."

"I won't budge! I won't let you work!"

"Oh, yeah?" I don't want to do it, but I see I've got no choice. The window is open and I push Poindexter toward it. He spreads his bat-like wings, but he can't get his balance long enough to take flight.

"This is going to hurt you more than it hurts me," I grin.

Suddenly I'm not so sure. Poindexter whacks me one with the arm coming out of his forehead. The quills sting.

But we're at the window now, and I push hard. Out he goes. "Good riddance!" I shout.

His twelve puke-green eyes look scared for a moment. Then, halfway down to the sidewalk he gets his bat wings spread and takes flight.

"I'll be back!" he threatens as he heads for the sky.

"I'll be ready!" I promise.

Don't worry about doing this exercise "correctly"; just do it. The only rule, whether you write a full-blown scene or use a dialogue, is that *you win*. Even winning can take a variety of forms: You can violently destroy the Beast, or you can reach more of a compromise, e.g., Poindexter sits quietly for an hour in a corner of the room and lets you get some work done.

Use this as an opportunity to be a little wild and crazy. You're not writing for publication, or for anyone else to read it, so let loose. Put the exercise away and look at it again tomorrow. You may be surprised to find that you've written a darn good dialogue or scene.

The Worse-Case Scenario

Here is another exercise for breaking through the barriers you may have erected for yourself.

Imagine that the thing you fear most actually happens. Write about that. Write it as a scene, though, rather than just describing your abstract emotions. An example of the latter would be: "I am afraid of failure. I am afraid of feeling bad about myself. I am afraid that people will laugh at me, and the worst things my father ever thought about me will be true."

Without more, these statements of your fears, may just reinforce your belief in them. So instead, look at how you can translate the fears personified by the Beast into concrete *events*, complete with actions, dialogue and sensory details. Write about a terrible, feared occurrence in the past tense, as if it had already happened.

Here is one:

> The mail came every day at 10:20. For some reason, Bruce, the mailman, was late that day. I had already been out on the porch thirteen times. I hoped the neighbors weren't watching from their windows — they'd guess how desperate I was. The first five times I was still in my bathrobe, but then I forced myself to put on a pair of jeans and a clean T-shirt.
>
> When I saw Bruce coming down the street, pushing his mail sack on those little wheels, I could tell just from the way he whistled that I was in trouble. It was a sunny day, at least 70°, but when I saw him I got goose bumps on my arms from the sudden chill I felt.
>
> "Got another one of them boxes for you," Bruce said cheerfully, coming up my steps. When he grinned, I could see his chipped front tooth. "You sure get a lot of these!"
>
> "Thanks." I smiled, so he wouldn't know to feel sorry for me, and reluctantly unfolded my freezing arms from my chest.
>
> "See ya tomorrow. Maybe I'll even have another box." Bruce trotted back down the steps and on to the next house, while I stood on my porch alone, staring at my novel. Another publisher had sent it back.

Here's another example:

> My wife and I were at breakfast when I stumbled on the review. Well, that will teach me to read the *Wall Street Journal!*
>
> "It's hard to believe this travesty of fiction was ever published," the reviewer had written about my first novel, *Let the Yellowbird Sing.*
>
> The phone rang all morning. I got calls from my editor, my agent, and everyone at the office, supposedly offering sympathy.
>
> "You must feel really awful," Fred Granger said. Fred and I belonged to the same health club, and he'd always been threatened by my writing, besides not being able to swim as many laps as I could.

Your fears, like some fungi, thrive in the moist, dark corners of your mind. Dragged out into the light, with the bright sun of your words shining on them, they wither. Writing about them, you will begin to feel more confident that you can survive rejections, bad reviews, the envy of your friends, the unforgiving light of publicity.

But even more important (though maybe I shouldn't tell you this), you will also be *writing*. You will be practicing the use of language, learning to observe and to invent details, and you'll probably enjoy it.

You may also find it inspiring to write about some of the good things that might happen. Write about your first book signing, about getting fan mail, or about being profiled in your hometown newspaper.

The Right Things

Affirmations are currently a popular tool for self-improvement, but we should try not to hold that against them.

An affirmation is a statement of desired belief or behavior that a person writes, says or listens to to reinforce that belief or behavior. (Therapists call this "cognitive restructuring.")

The author Brad Newsham describes how he does the following affirmation, "I am in exactly the right place, thinking, doing and feeling exactly the right things." He writes that sentence ten times a day. (His first book was titled, *All the Right Places*.)

Affirmations are especially suited to writers. When the masses do affirmations, they have to scrabble around to find a regular time to do them; we, however, were planning to sit down to write anyway.

As a bonus, the affirmation is a painless thing to sit down to. In other words, when you head over to your desk, you know you don't have to be brilliantly creative the first moment you hit the chair. You can write somewhat mindlessly for a few minutes, get used to the pen in your hand or the keys under your fingertips, as your mind begins to pick up the threads of what you were working on the day before.

During tough writing times, or when you're starting out and only working for those magical, but mandatory, ten minutes a day, affirmations count as the "something—anything," you can write during those ten minutes, as we discussed in chapter three.

Here are some other affirmations you might try:

"I, (your name), am a brilliant writer who is writing a successful novel."

"I write effortlessly every day."

"I love to write and I concentrate fully on my work."

Brad Newsham also says about his affirmations, "I listen to the voice in my head [the Beast] that assures me I am worthless, or whatever it is assuring me that day. And I write an affirmation to counter that thought."

So invent your own affirmations, according to your needs. If you are afraid that everyone will hate your novel, write ten times, "I know that everyone will love my novel."

Make your affirmations positive. Instead of repeating, "My work isn't stupid," write, "My work is very intelligent." And do write the affirmations, as opposed to simply saying them aloud. It's another way to drum it into your own head that you're a writer.

Making affirmations a part of your daily routine may be something that works for you. Even if you don't fully believe, at that moment, in the affirmation you are writing, you are telling yourself to believe it. Over time, it starts to sink in.

More Help Available

If, after trying all of these exercises, you still want to write but continue to feel so conflicted that somehow you just can't, then you might consider talking to a counselor or therapist, especially one who specializes in working with artists. There is absolutely no shame in doing so. Keep in mind that the most talented and successful writers get blocked. On the other hand (as you know only too well, if you are blocked), there is nothing romantic about being afraid to write, and you don't want to waste any more time than necessary on it. Go talk to someone soon.

Meanwhile, keep reading this book. There are more ideas ahead. In my experience, we never know what word, suggestions or technique might suddenly turn us loose.

TO GET THAT NOVEL STARTED

Identify the fears that may be in your way

and then get them out *of your way.*

CHAPTER FIVE

The Idea Bank

Unanswerable Questions

People often ask me, "Where do you get your ideas?" I'm never sure how to answer. This is one of those times, though, when I'm tempted to do a little artistic posing. "They just *come* to me," I want to reply, as if I have my very own Idea Fairy, a sweet little Tinkerbell who visits my software.

Sometimes the ideas do just come to you. You're looking for a solution, and there it is, and you have cause to celebrate.

But my purpose, in part, with this book, is to demystify writing. It isn't helpful to talk about how "it just happens, no one knows how," because that means that all of us who want to write novels will sit around and wait for them to happen to us, as if novels were earthquakes that struck without warning.

The Well

I believe that all of us have an unlimited amount of ideas within us. They're just there. What we need to practice — and can acquire — is the skill of *accessing* those ideas.

So, when I suggest ways to get ideas, what I am really suggesting are methods of looking at the big world around you to find associations: sparks that ignite something within. There are unlimited sources of material, and we can learn to look outside to see what matches up with our inner needs, compulsions and desires to discover what issues compel us enough to write novels about them.

The story and the ideas we eventually find will be the ones we were looking for all along.

Now, About Those Ideas

You will develop your own favorite sources. Here are some of mine and some other writers:

The Morning Newspaper

Don't look just at the headlines; read the more obscure, and often more offbeat, items that are buried in the middle pages or the feature sections.

Some examples from today's *San Francisco Chronicle*:

1. Ear piercing has become passé among teenagers, who prefer to punch holes for jewelry in other parts of their bodies. (What if your teenage character came home with a ring in her nose?)

2. Cooking meat at high temperature seems to increase the risk of cancer. (What if your married couple, already troubled, had another fight because of the husband's refusal to barbecue for the rest of the summer?)

3. Thieves stole a 1,700-pound automated teller machine from a concrete enclosure outside a bank. (So *that's* the crime your detective has to solve!)

Martin Cruz Smith's *Gorky Park* and Judith Rossner's *Looking for Mr. Goodbar*, both best-sellers, were inspired by real-life incidents.

Don't overlook Ann Landers and Dear Abby, either — every day they contain enough human drama to fill a week of "As the World Turns."

The Boob Tube

Newsmagazines, such as "60 Minutes" or even the tabloid shows, are often about interesting people and occurrences that may lead to other ideas for your fiction: a profile of a nun who founded a shelter for the homeless, or the scandal surrounding a politician's investment in a poorly run old-age home.

Any television program can be a source of inspiration though. My sister and I were hard-core fans of the prime-time soap opera "Dallas." Some years back, the end-of-the-season cliff-hanger came when Cliff (no pun intended) Barnes was rushed to the hospital after a suicide attempt. Sue Ellen Ewing, his current flame, rushed to see the comatose Cliff breathing through a respirator just before the closing credits.

That night, as I was falling asleep, I imagined the disembodied spirit of a comatose woman, hovering above her bed, watching herself breathe through a respirator as her family gathered around. That was the germ image of my first published novel, *Extraordinary Means*.

I haven't forgotten that I said that television was the enemy of writing time. But we all need to zone out occasionally, so if you find yourself in front of the set, use television as a source of ideas, or to study plot structure. A few TV shows are fast-paced and well put together, and there is no shortage of dramatic events.

At the same time, keep in mind that television deals in broad concepts, sensationalism and sentimentality. Don't let overexposure numb you to the finer nuances of character and emotion that you must also attune yourself to as a novelist.

Nonfiction

What subjects do you like to read about? All writers should read as much as possible. There are no "shoulds" about the topics — you are more likely to find inspiration in subjects that appeal to you. As a fiction writer, you have a natural inclination to use what you know or learn about; this is the writer's impulse. Reading about a subject that interests you, you're not only getting ideas, you're also painlessly researching. (My interest in psychoanalysis led me to write *California Street*, a mystery about an analyst.)

Your favorite period of history can become the setting for a historical novel, an ever-popular genre. I've always been fascinated by the Tudor monarchs and have fantasized writing a novel set in the court of Henry VIII or Elizabeth I.

Be open-minded. Back to the subject of psychoanalysis, Freud described a state of "calm, quiet attentiveness — 'evenly-hovering' attention," which left the analyst most open to pick out the clues from a patient's free associations. If, when you read, you are frantically hunting for the perfect idea, you may miss it. Believe it will come to you, and it will.

The old writing adage goes, "Write what you know." I believe you should write what you *want*. If you don't "know" about what you want to write about, then study it.

Interviews

People interested in pursuing a new career are often advised to seek out "informational interviews": a visit with a practicing professional to find out what that professional does. You will want to do the same with people who work in the field that your characters work in. If you are writing about a computer programmer, unless you are or have been one yourself, you are well-advised to speak to one or more computer programmers about how they spend their days.

Use this technique even if you don't know what you are writing about yet. Talk to a doctor about his patients, a lawyer about her cases. Listening to these and other professionals' "war stories," you will also catch some of their passions and their frustrations with their work.

I once had a very funny conversation with a shoe saleslady who described to me how she could tell, when a customer first walked in, who would spend two hours looking without buying anything, and who would walk out with $600 worth of shoes only to return them the following day.

So talk to the people you know about what they do—not just their careers, but their pastimes. Or ask your grandmother about some of the more colorful incidents of her childhood. You've probably been meaning to anyway.

Strangers in the Day

It is perfectly legitimate, when your writing time comes, to head down to the park and sit yourself on a bench with a notebook on your lap and observe passersby.

Make up stories about them. That elderly lady with the fraying plastic bag from Kmart. Where does she live? What did she eat for breakfast? Do her children ever visit her?

Try the same thing with the people at your bus stop, or in line with you at the grocery store.

Eavesdrop on someone's conversation in a public place. Fill in the gaps yourself. Who is the mysterious "Phil" that the blonde woman is so worried about? And why *won't* he get himself a new apartment?

Get Involved

Seek out new experiences. Your writer's impulse will push you to recount those experiences to others in turn, in the hopes they will share your perceptions of them.

When I was working, years ago, at a crisis hotline, I wrote a one-act play about people at a crisis hotline. When I went to Paris to spend a year, I wrote about living in Paris.

Take a camping trip. Eat dehydrated food and wrestle with an easy-to-assemble tent. Then the couple in your novel can have the same adventures.

Just don't get too busy to write.

Other Arts

Studying other forms of self-expression will always add dimension to your writing. Try taking a photography, dance or acting class. You don't have to become Ansel Adams or Cynthia Gregory, but besides getting out for a night (though see "Get Involved," above, for the dangers of getting out for *too* many nights), you will learn how a photographer composes shapes, how a dancer stretches, and how an actor reaches within himself, all in the service of making something new.

Writers get very hung up on words. That's understandable because they're our only real equipment. The danger is that we become so cerebral that we lose touch with the wordless, emotional sources of our work. Our responses to the performing and visual arts tend to be more visceral.

Go to a museum. Look at how a conceptual artist makes a sculpture out of bent nails from a construction site, or hats from a Salvation Army store. Who knows, you may end up writing about a conceptual artist.

Durable Fictions

How often have you heard something described as "a Cinderella story"? The classic plots get used over and over, and you, too, can look to them for inspiration.

James Joyce used the structure of the epic poem the "Odyssey" as the basis of his equally epic work, *Ulysses.*

John Gardner retold the story of *Beowulf* from the point of view of the monster and called it *Grendel.*

Steve Martin, in his film *Roxanne*, retold the story of *Cyrano de Bergerac*, setting it in modern British Columbia.

You don't have to pay such close homage to the original of a favorite story. If you read a lot of mysteries, though, you will get ideas for mysteries of your own; likewise if you read sea adventures, vampire novels or westerns.

The Bottom Line (Is Your Bottom on a Chair)

As always, the most important thing is to keep writing, *because your best ideas will come to you after you have sat down, not an idea in your head, and started to write about nothing.* The writer and teacher Natalie Goldberg repeatedly emphasizes how important it is to "keep your hand moving." Go back to chapter three and review the list of suggestions for "jump-starters."

When we are at the stage of getting ideas, we must put our need to judge the value of those ideas on hold. Ignore the Beast when it tells you, "You can't write about a secretary, that's too boring," or "It's too cliché to have your main character fall in love with her sister's husband." Both may be, but you can't know that until you hang out with the idea for a little while.

If you continually draw blanks, or don't get ideas at all, then you may be dismissing thoughts before they even reach the level of your awareness. Go back and do the exercises outlined in chapter four.

In fact, there are no sure-winner ideas. Your job as a novelist is to make your ideas interesting to the reader. The writer's impulse I've mentioned is your desire to do just that.

Organizing Your Ideas

This is the fun part, first of all because it gives you an excuse to head down to the stationery store and browse.

Pick out something you love: a sleek, black three-ring binder with pastel-ruled paper. Or go for colored index cards (I love the way they make everything multi-colored these days). Get some cute index tabs and an adorable little file box.

Divide your loose-leaf notebook paper or your file cards into various headings. Try:

Characters

This can be anything about people. Write down names for characters that occur to you—"Lois Broadway"or "Petra Lembecke."

Write down physical characteristics you observe—the butcher's bulbous, red-veined nose, or the tight curve of your baby's toe.

This heading might also include funny things that people say, or a terribly witty riposte you made the other night (or you can make a separate heading for dialogue).

Events (or "Story Ideas")

These might come from any of the above sources. Maybe the morning paper tells the story of a bomb scare that disrupted a parade, or a newly crowned beauty queen who displayed a sign declaring that beauty pageants exploited women. Maybe you have *no idea* how these events will fit in your novel; maybe they never will. But if they intrigue you—because of the rage you feel at the former and the amusement you feel at the latter—put them down.

Fragments

These are the flashes of insight that come to you as you wait for your tea to brew or you walk down the street. Perhaps as you look at the grass sprouting through the cracks in the sidewalk, it reminds you of your grandfather's eyebrows. Write that down.

Research

This is where you can make a note of questions you need to answer. No matter how closely you stick to subjects you know about, your story will pose questions that need answering, be it a first aid procedure or a bus route. You can also note down the answers here, when you get them.

Create any other headings that you find useful. You'll make deposits in your idea bank, and you'll have a place to go make withdrawals. Americans should save more.

Carry a small notebook with you to jot down ideas or observations that you can transfer to your three-ring binder or card file later. Keep the notebook by your bed at night. (You may have gotten in this habit when you started collecting jump-starters, as suggested in chapter three.) Then you can tear out pages of the notebook and put them in pocket files if you don't want to spend a lot of time recopying them.

Sure, your filing system will get messy. Who said writing a novel was neat? When your categories blur, that means you are entering your novel more deeply, getting to that place where characters and story are inseparable, just like they are in life.

The Best Source of All

The most obvious, the most frequently used, and the richest source of ideas is one's own life—but it's also the touchiest, so it deserves a separate discussion.

For most of us, this is what we *want* to write about. Our sad childhoods and sweet mothers, our lost loves and slow recoveries, our tough choices and personal triumphs. What could ever compel us more?

In chapter four, we discussed some of the inhibitions that may get in the way of our writing about our true material. Our true material will, by definition, be the scariest and the most difficult to write about, but if we avoid it and try to find something safer, our writing will reflect that avoidance. Our words will be less certain, our insights unconvincing.

One thing that scares us about writing about our own life is the self-exposure. We want to "express" ourselves (the writer's impulse again), but we also want to control the flow of information. Too much control, at least on the level of content, is death to our writing. Consciously or not, the reader senses our fear, our need for approval.

Sure, you can also overwhelm the reader with self-pity disguised as art. No one wants to read 300 pages of pure moaning about how mean your parents were and how mad you are about it. That's why only very famous people or extremely insightful writers publish their journals.

By far the more common occurrence is the writer who hopes to move people to tears and laughter without taking any risks herself. She may hesitate to write about the pain of a little girl being teased about her buckteeth on the playground for fear of herself being perceived as homely and pathetic, especially if it *really did happen*.

Don't hold back. Remember that, if your "true material" is really incendiary, you always have the option of publishing under a pseudonym. Most of us don't want to, though—when we finally rise from the typewriter with our shaking hands and bloodshot eyes, we want people to know that we're the ones who did the work.

Fair Game

And what about writing about others you know? If your brother once confided to you that, while in medical school, he plagiarized another student's paper for his anatomy class, and he made you promise never to reveal his secret, then you don't want to depict that event in your novel in such a way that he feels betrayed (or gets kicked out of school).

But when you put your writer hat on, you should be daring, willing to expose yourself, and willing to write about what you find dramatic and compelling.

Take off the gloves. Be ruthless. (An editor once said to me, "You may not be a nice person, but you're a good writer." I was flattered.)

This book is not meant to substitute for any legal advice you feel you might need if you are writing about controversial, true-to-life events. In general, though, you can feel free to fictionalize almost anything. The key word is "fictionalize."

There are ways to disguise even very distressing, personal events so that you and others involved can feel safer. You can write about someone stealing a paper without saying, "This is my brother, folks." The male medical student can become a female Ph.D. candidate who plagiarizes another student's work on Lawrence Durrell.

Or, let's say a character in your novel is based on your brother, who in real life has a little trouble following the rules. You feel it's important to the dramatization of your character that you depict some of your brother's transgressions, which have given real pain to others. In real life, your brother has not only plagiarized other students' work, he has pilfered the occasional hubcap, and more or less invented his résumés when looking for a summer job.

Your fictional brother could travel the same unethical road—only he uses a fake name to log onto the computer, tells his girl-friend he's at home studying when he's actually out with *her* girl-friend, and "borrows" your uncle's American Express card for a weekend away.

Seeing Ourselves as Others See Us

I said in chapter four that you may be surprised to discover how slow people are to recognize themselves in your writing. That's because our self-image differs so greatly from the perceptions of others. Often a trait that most annoys you in someone else—a nervous tic or even an abiding selfishness—is something that person is completely unaware of. (Often, too, the qualities we find most disturbing or admirable in someone else match up with parts of ourselves we reject or embrace, so in writing about these others, we are actually revealing our own internal struggles.)

I cannot, unfortunately, reassure you that no one will ever give you any flak. Of course, everyone who knows you will be looking for themselves in what you write—so much so that sometimes people will accuse you of betraying their secrets in a character's quirks when nothing could have been further from your mind: You didn't even *know* that your friend Wilma flossed her teeth four times a day when you decided to make that a charming idiosyncrasy of your heroine.

Since you can't protect yourself completely anyway, you might as well write about the real people and events you want to write about.

Keep in mind that your readers will be looking for externals. Your paper-stealing, résumé-fudging brother will be looking for "the brother" in your novel, or the character who resembles him physically, more than he will be looking for a young man with shaky morals.

If your brother is tall and dark-haired, wears a mustache and bites his nails, those are the traits he will immediately identify with. Describe your character you've based on him as a short, blond, chain-smoker and you automatically create distance between the real and the fictional man.

Sure, if your brother is a smart guy, he'll guess what you're up to. His own sense of exposure, though, will be minimized by these surface changes.

It's Fiction, Folks

Let's extend this to an entire novel. Suppose your father was in the Army, and as children you and your sister had to move frequently. That caused you a lot of unhappiness, something you've never had the nerve to talk to your parents about.

Maybe you've been thinking, well, I'll wait 'til they die, then write a poignant novel about the suffering of a couple of Army brats.

Don't wait! Your parents should live long and happy lives, and you shouldn't deprive them of the pleasure of seeing you publish a novel. Write the book, and make some changes in the story that don't affect the emotional content. Give the main character a brother instead of a sister, or two sisters. Change the order of the Army bases that the family lives in, or change the Army to the Navy.

Some changes will feel more comfortable than others to you as the author. You may want to write about the particular dynamic that exists between two sisters, so that adding a sibling to your fictional family is too jarring to your concept of the novel. Fine — there are plenty of other things you can change.

As suggested earlier, it's often a good idea to change the physical appearances of the characters. Physical appearance certainly affects who a character is, and if you change the character inspired by your Aunt Edith from slim and tiny-featured, to obese and stragglyhaired, you will have created a person different from her prototype. Changing physical characteristics is an excellent way to disguise them.

Choose a name for your fictional character right away; this is the beginning of a new life for him or her. Then change other externals, especially ones that happen to be less relevant to the story you want to tell. If the teacher you hated in the eleventh grade taught algebra, switch her over to French. Let her torture you over irregular verbs, instead of logarithms.

Artistically, this is a good move as well. I said that we want to write about our own lives, and we should. But it's one thing to be inspired by real-life people who affected you; it's another to be so committed to "reality" that you miss dramatic opportunities or ignore the call of your imagination to create characters who live and breathe (metaphorically speaking) on their own.

It's also rare that what really happened—*exactly* as it happened, anyway—is interesting enough for a novel. Generally, you need to hit the high points: You won't describe every single audition you went to before you became a movie star, or every single experiment you helped construct before you discovered a cure for cancer. Feel free, as a novelist, to shape the facts into a more dramatic and aesthetic whole.

Disguise-a-Character

Change some things; leave some things the same.

Hillary	Renée
5′3″	5′9″
Brunette	Blonde
Legal Secretary	Legal Secretary
Secret Ambition:	Secret Ambition:
Writer	Performance Artist
Drives VW Bug	Drives Pinto
Lives in Log Angeles	Lives in Los Angeles
Boyfriend:	Boyfriend:
Electrician Named Bob	Musician Named "Free"

The Family in the Novel

The reverse of everything above is also true. If you want people to recognize themselves, you can make sure that they do.

My first novel was semi-autobiographical. The protagonist, Melissa, came from an upper-middle-class family, was the daughter of warring parents, had a loving but *noodgy* grandmother, and was the oldest child, which was all true of me, too.

I changed many things, as well. Among them: In the book, Melissa has a brother and two sisters, while I have only two sisters. More tellingly, perhaps, Melissa's parents, though they have a turbulent relationship, are still married, while my own parents divorced when I was seven.

These changes fit the story I was writing, but I didn't make any pretense that the characters weren't inspired by my own family. After all, although I gave each character a fictional name, I was writing about A Mother, A Father, Two Sisters, etc. I knew very well that when my mother, father and sisters read the novel they would recognize anything that *did* come from life. Still, I typed happily away, aided in this case by my underlying disbelief that the book would really be published.

The thud of a box of advance copies landing at my door ended my denial. And then, since God gives special radar to all parents, my father showed up within hours to claim his copy. As soon as it was available in stores, the rest of my family followed suit.

Everyone seemed to feel kind of creepy about it at first, including me. It was as if we'd been taped for a PBS special. When my mother finished reading it, she called me up in tears. But within a week, not only did everyone's discomfort evaporate, it changed to pride. My father bought six copies to give to friends; my mother loaned hers out to anyone who would read it.

No one stopped speaking to me; no one has written scathing rebuttals. In fact, things are pretty much the same between my parents and me, and my sisters and me, as they always were — both the good and the bad. Writing the book didn't erase any of the hurts of my childhood, anymore than it inflamed them. What did change, with that book, is that I became a novelist, and being a novelist is central to my life now.

Everyone can survive the writing of a novel. You, too.

TO GET THAT NOVEL STARTED

Start collecting ideas, and then start writing about them. Don't worry about whether the ideas are right, wrong, good, bad, "made up" or "true."

PART TWO

The Taming of the Novel

CHAPTER SIX

Are We Writing Yet?

Ready, Set, Write!

You've got some daily writing time. You've dealt with the writer's normal fears — or at least hounded them into the corner for the moment. You've got a card file bursting with brilliant ideas and fragments. You've got a new word processor or a sharp pencil. You're ready.

What next?

For purposes of this and later chapters, I will use an invented, sample novel, *Mommies Don't Cry*, to illustrate how a general idea can evolve into an outline and an opening scene.

The Basic Idea

Write down your novel idea, as much of it as you know. That may be one sentence — "something about my first marriage" — or it may be several pages.

I'm going to write down all I know about my idea for *Mommies Don't Cry* at this moment:

> I want to write a book about my first year as a mother. I want to capture all the wonder of watching a new human being come into the world, along with the complete shock of having one's entire lifestyle go through such dramatic changes.
>
> I'll give the main character a husband, and he'll be sort of like my own husband, but I'll find some things to change, too, so that my real-life husband won't feel embarrassed.
>
> One of the things I'm most interested in writing about is in the woman's relationship with the baby-sitter. I don't

think that gets written about much — how dependent you can get on a good sitter, not just for practical reasons, but because she becomes like a substitute mother to you, too.

I'll begin when the main character, the mother, goes into labor, and describe the birth. Then I'll describe how she has to go back to work and how hard that is. Maybe she and her husband will have some problems. It'll all end happily — or at least, she'll start to feel more secure about raising a child.

As you write down your idea, more thoughts will occur to you, so write those down, too.

Here's something else: Maybe I can put the couple into a new house, too, so that while the wife is having to adjust to being a mother, she and her husband are also dealing with appliances that don't work and painters going in and out.

I guess the wife/mother will need a best friend to confide in, so I'll base that character on my friend Debbie.

I'll even make my main character a novelist, so I can write about what that's like.

Take a few days to continue to expand the basic idea. Put down anything you want about it — possible titles, incidents — all the things you've been thinking about. A lot of what you write down will not end up in the final novel, but this is not the time to edit — this is the time to let things flow.

If you have more than one idea, go ahead and write what you know about each of them. Then, choose an idea that you can commit to. It's certainly worth spending a little time at this stage to consider which one that will be. Don't base your choice on what you think will be the easiest to write, and don't be too influenced by what you think will be the most salable. Go ahead and take both of these factors into account — there's nothing wrong with writing a manageable, easy-to-sell novel, especially your first time out — as long as you consider what themes, settings and events you feel the most passionate about.

There is a practical reason for this: A novel will probably take you a minimum of a year, and a number of hours that few of us have the nerve to calculate. There's little point in attempting it, with all its frustrations, rewrites and dull stretches, unless the subject matter is something you can relate to and care about. Your passion for that subject will help you see through the tougher times.

The author Donna Gillespie once described to me how people pushed her so hard to write contemporary short stories, that it took her a year before she finally had the nerve to embark upon the book she truly wanted to write. *The Light Bearer*, her first novel, is set in first-century Rome and Germania; Gillespie re-creates these places so lovingly and relentlessly that they're both as real and dream-like as the Manhattan of Woody Allen's films.

Fortunately, there are a lot of readers, a lot of authors, and a lot of subjects. You get to choose.

The Myth of the Easy Novel

I want quickly to dispense with yet another of those insidious little writing myths going around, which is that some authors "cop out" to write best-sellers, as if best-sellers were easy little volumes to dash off.

A student in a class of mine once observed that a very famous and popular novelist had met with her success because, "She doesn't care if she writes a good book," to which I replied, "Then we should all stop caring so much!"

Popular fiction isn't easier or harder than "serious" fiction. It is true that purely popular, rather than more literary, fiction generally relies more heavily on fast pacing and plot twists, than on original characterizations or lyrical prose, and books like these are more likely to be about rich people living in glamour capitals than about immigrants struggling to farm the land.

But that doesn't make them easier. If best-sellers required only cynicism and a few months of your life, the best-seller list would be longer than the Encyclopedia Brittanica.

Write the best book you can write. Study the authors who write books you admire, be that Thomas Wolfe's *Look Homeward, Angel*, or Sidney Sheldon's *Rage of Angels*. You should play to your strengths, but you shouldn't dismiss a good plot as the stuff of potboilers anymore than you should neglect the masterful use of language as the indulgence of poets or academics.

No one can predict what will make the best-seller list. Follow the idea that calls to you; it will take you the furthest.

And if nothing seems to be calling—or all you hear are a few mumbles—well, that's okay, too. Just move on to the next step:

Who's Who and What to Call Them

Choose your "protagonist," or main character.

Now you can no longer be stuck, because you can use your

partner or your best friend or one of your parents as the inspiration for your main character. If you are an unmarried orphan with no friends, you can always use yourself.

Give this main character a name. As we discussed in chapter five, no matter how closely you plan to stick to "reality" (a fluid concept if ever there was one, in any case) it's important to give yourself and your characters freedom to grow. Naming them is like giving birth to them, so do that right away. You'll change many characters' names as you go, but it's an important first step.

The significance of names is deeply imbedded in us. A religious confirmant takes a new name, to symbolize his or her rebirth in Christ. Some primitive peoples believed that knowing someone's true name gave you power over them. Our modern version of that belief is demonstrated by researchers who attempt to show that a child's name determines his future success or failure in life: that a Robert has greater prospects than a Melvin.

When Jack Rosenberg changed his name to Werner Erhard, when Cassius Clay became Muhammed Ali, and when Samuel Clemens became Mark Twain, their personae changed, too.

Some authors — particularly in the mystery and romance genres — invent names that grab us immediately because of their unusualness: "Chantal DuBarry" or "Quinby Mortimer." These are fun for you and the reader, at least up to the point where the proliferation of exotic combinations strains credibility.

Science fiction authors may choose names to indicate who in our current day will be important in the future. Aldous Huxley peopled his classic, *Brave New World*, with names like Benito (after Benito Mussolini), Lenina (after Vladimir Lenin) and Darwin (after Charles Darwin).

Watch out for "Ozzie and Harriet" names. On the old "Ozzie and Harriet" show, guest characters usually had names like Ann Parker or Cathy Johnson, that is, names that were extremely common and completely devoid of any ethnicity.

When I was in elementary school, reading young adult fiction, all the characters in the books had "Ozzie and Harriet" names. This was a tunnel-vision time, when most children's literature did not acknowledge anyone without an Anglo-Saxon name. (Often, too, you hear names like these in movies, where the name of the character is far less significant to the audience than the movie star playing the part.)

Obviously, a name like Ann Parker, or even John Smith, conveys certain things about that character. (John Smith would remind us of the explorer rescued by Pocahontas, or make us think of old jokes about couples checking into motels anonymously.) There's nothing wrong with a popular Anglo-Saxon name. Just be aware that an entire novel peopled by "Ozzie and Harriet" refugees will seem false, unless you intend to satirize that kind of world, the same way a large cast of characters with names like Tiffany, Alexandra and Gwendolyn will sound like an afternoon soap.

You don't have to make sure that each name you choose has an appropriate Latin meaning and a pedigree of similarly called heroes or heroines. Find a name that sounds right to you, that you want to listen to for a while. But do consider the connotation of different names. "Daisy" seems appropriate for the flower-like heroine of *The Great Gatsby*, just as "Tom" does for her philandering (i.e., "tomcat") husband. Margaret Mitchell's original name for the heroine of *Gone With the Wind* was "Pansy," but "Scarlett" (as in "scarlet woman") certainly does the job much better. You can play against type in a name, too: "Mary" conveys innocence and purity, so it might be interesting to use for a conniving female character, just as it would be ironic to give a lumberjack the name Francis or Blair.

Sources for names include but are hardly limited to: the phone book, a baby name book, names you can remember from your elementary school, and characters from other books you like. Mix and match first and last names, of course.

I'm going to call the protagonist of *Mommies Don't Cry* "Robin." It's a name I like, and evokes something little, cute and flighty; a creature who might be stunned by motherhood.

For a last name I'll use Decker, just to have something to start with. That's her married name—it has a more masculine sound. I'll come up with a maiden name for her later.

Don't get hung up on this step any more than any other. Play with names, have some fun, then pick one and move on. Once again: you can always change them, just like you can change everything.

The Story of Your Who

Now, write a biography of your main character. (Ten to fifteen pages is a good guideline for the main character; five to ten will do when you get to secondary characters.) Focus on the main events that shape a person's life. Answer at least the following questions:

1. Was his/her childhood happy or unhappy? (And why, specifically?)
2. Where did he or she grow up?
3. What were his or her first romantic encounters like?
4. How much education does he or she have?

As your biography catches up with the character's current age, get more detailed about recent love affairs, friends, problems and personal accomplishments—these recent events will more likely impact the character or figure in the action of the novel.

Conclude with a thorough description of the character's present life. Sketch his or her physical appearance, and decide where he or she currently lives (and with whom, if anyone), and how he or she supports him or herself. Consider as well:

1. Who are the most important people in this person's life and how does she feel about them?
2. What is the biggest problem she faces?
3. How does she feel about herself? How does she see herself in the world? (A speck tossed about by random chance or a future savior of mankind?)

Those are the biggies, but of course you want to add any other information you can think of. How does this person dress? (Does she wear old jeans and T-shirts to the office, or high heels around the house? Does he have his suits tailor-made or buy slacks at Goodwill?) What does she like to eat—tofu or potato chips? What's his favorite TV show? Does the character vote Republican, Democrat, Libertarian, or not at all?

As an exercise, you can come up with a whole list of offbeat questions to answer about your character, like what her favorite color is, or when her birthday is, or what her favorite sports teams are. Don't try to save yourself time by limiting yourself to what you "need" to know. None of what you learn will be wasted, although many of the details you invent won't show up in the novel itself. Writing a biography is like sitting down to get to know someone, and the better you know that person, the more convincingly you will write about her.

Here's a short sample bio for Robin Decker.

Robin was born in San Francisco, at Children's Hospital. She grew up in the Richmond District and went to Washington High. Her mother was a full-time housewife, and her father was a lawyer. She's the middle child; she has an older brother and a younger sister.

Robin's family was always comfortable enough financially, but she was lonely, especially as a teenager. She has the "middle child syndrome": The older brother, Jim, had the distinction of being the only son, and he was a star student besides. The younger sister, Amy, got attention for being the baby, and later, she was always embroiled in some sort of drama — either a teacher didn't like her or she was fighting with her boyfriend. Robin was the quiet, well-behaved one, with the result that she was often ignored, and it's made her shy and insecure.

Her parents wanted her to go into something with science or computers. "That's the future," they always said. But Robin majored in English at Stanford and now she's a writer, mostly of film criticism. (She's always loved movies as a form of escape.)

Robin didn't date much in high school. In college she fell in with a close-knit group of artsy types who liked coffeehouses and Bergman revivals. She had no serious relationship with a man until she met her husband, Paul.

Robin graduated from college with honors and fully intended to go on for a graduate degree either in journalism or creative writing. But she was offered a job on a small weekly magazine in San Francisco, and she decided to work there for a year just to get experience. Eventually she worked her way up to become film reviewer for the magazine (I'll call it *HERE* magazine), a job that isn't particularly high-paying but that has a patina of glamour: she gets invited to screenings and to parties with film people. (She writes under her maiden name: Sovicki. There; it's not a particularly feminine name, but I like it for being so different from Decker.) She also teaches a course in film criticism at a local community college.

When she was thirty, her boss at the magazine introduced her to Paul. They were married within a year, after a very romantic courtship — Sunday brunches, long walks in the park, evening sailboat rides.

Paul is two years older than Robin, an ambitious and hardworking stockbroker. When she married him, she felt she had attained a kind of specialness that she never felt in her own family. In fact, she has some ambivalence about standing out, which should explain both why she has this job she loves and yet hasn't been able to fulfill deeper ambitions, to move on to a more prestigious magazine, or to write a serious book about film.

Robin is 5'2"; slim, with short, straight dark brown hair and brown eyes. (She'd rather be called "petite" than "short.") She has clear olive skin, and a definite pug nose. She's more cute than beautiful. She's self-conscious about what she considers a weak chin (but actually it's not that bad).

Robin likes funky things—she likes to wear baggy pants and vests and men's shirts. She doesn't smoke, but she likes to collect ashtrays from places like the Holiday Inn or the IHOP.

Robin and Paul have been married three years, and live in San Francisco. They lived in a one-bedroom apartment in a high rise until Robin got pregnant, then they bought a small house. Robin was very excited about getting pregnant (it was an accident; she and Paul had planned to wait another year or two), but she is also fearful of what motherhood will do to her writing career, which is also very important to her.

Your biography will not only be much longer and more detailed, it won't be as neat or chronological; there will be lots of lines scratched out and there may be some gaps.

The initial notes you make about the main character will overlap with notes you made about the overall idea. That's good. (Keep collecting those pages!)

Do, however, be as specific as possible. If you say that a character is "good" or "disagreeable," be sure to say why—that he frequently visits his invalid grandmother or that she yells at the grocery clerk when he puts the bread at the bottom of the bag.

More Homework

Here are two additional exercises for getting to know your characters:

The Interview

Imagine you have your character in a chair across from you. Talk to him or her, and get right to the big questions.

Donna: So, Robin, what's your biggest problem right now?
Robin: Well, Donna, I guess my resemblance to the Good-

year blimp is kind of on my mind. You know, my baby's due in two months.

Donna: Do you have names picked out?

Robin: Jonathan for a boy and Caroline for a girl.

Donna: How do you feel about having a baby?

Robin: Excited and scared. I have absolutely no experience with babies. Most of my friends have been putting off parenthood, too. Then there's my sister, Amy—she has two kids, but when they were really little, she was living with her husband in Los Angeles. Now she's divorced and lives in San Francisco again.

And so on, expanding on, and fine-tuning, what you already know about this character.

You might particularly enjoy this exercise if you have a journalism background and have experience doing interviews. Imagine yourself as the Barbara Walters of fiction.

The Monologue

In this exercise, you take the first-person voice of the character, who then describes her own life. You can do this whether or not the character speaks to the reader in first person in the novel (for a definition of the first person, see the section on point of view later in this chapter).

Write in the present tense, and assume that the action of the novel has already begun.

Thus:

All my life it was Jimmy, Jimmy, Jimmy, or Amy, Amy, Amy. Since I got pregnant is the first time my mother's even called me to see how I was doing—usually she waits for me to call her. Even when I got married she didn't seem too excited. I think she didn't want Amy to feel bad, because Amy had just gotten a divorce.

But you know, Amy and I are close anyway. I've always admired her energy, her optimism. And right now, I'm relying on her for any information she can give me about babies, because she's had kids for a while.

Ever since Jonathan was born, things have been really different between me and Paul. It's better, in some ways. We have this really intense joint project—raising the baby—and it's really fascinating to look at Jonathan and see how he looks like both of us already. But we're both so tired at the end of the day that we just collapse into bed. We're never alone together; we never just talk about work or what's in the news or even our friends—it's always, "Do we need a new stroller? What kind of high chair should we get?"

I spend a lot of time talking to Arianna, the baby-sitter. It's amazing, we have nothing in common that I can think of and yet we can talk for hours. She's been taking care of babies for twenty years, so I respect what she has to say, but it's more than that—we just chat, you know, the way women can chat sometimes, the way men simply will *not* chat. They can watch football for eight days straight, but they can't figure out why you would want to tell them a story about something that happened to you in junior high.

You can do the interview or the monologue instead of writing the biography, but I recommend doing the biography first, and using the second two exercises as a way of digging even deeper into your characters' minds.

A Word of Warning

I have to emphasize that you shouldn't get too attached to the material in your homework. It might be worth my while to write all about Robin's and Paul's first date, or to relate the initial discussion they had about whether and when to have children, but even if I do write those scenes, they are unlikely to be necessary to my finished novel.

In other words, as you do these exercises, you will start to feel infatuated with the early events of your characters' lives. Realize that it's only puppy love.

The Rest of the Cast and What They Want

Another advantage of the biography is that, while writing it, you will discover many possible secondary characters, some of whom will deserve their own biographies (and/or interviews and monologues), even though you may not yet know how largely they will figure in the book. Writing their biographies is one way of finding out whether you are interested enough in them to include them. No, you don't have to spend a week contemplating the motivations of a waitress who speaks one line, but we will meet a fair number of people in the course of a novel, and each of them should emerge as an individual.

Let's assume that we've done this background work for the cast of *Mommies*, and so briefly sketch the following characters:

ROBIN, the wife, 34.

PAUL, the husband, 36. He's a sports freak and a hard worker. He's a compassionate man, but he gets embarrassed talking about anything emotional, and he tends to withdraw when he feels threatened.

JONATHAN, the baby boy. Mildly colicky. Likes to nurse.

ARIANNA, 48, the baby-sitter Robin hires when she goes back to work (she does some of her writing at home). Arianna is originally from Patras, a small town in Greece. She's very experienced with babies and a bit domineering about the way things should be done; this plays on Robin's insecurities. She's very dark, with a broad nose and mouth; she and Robin look like they could be related.

AMY, 31, Robin's younger sister. She has two children, Jennie, 7, and Toby, 5. She survives on alimony, help from Robin's parents, and a series of ill-fated jobs (she recently started a fashion consulting service that didn't last long). She goes from one intense romance to the next.

FRANCES, Robin's mother, 59. When her kids left home, Frances went back to school, took up pottery, and now spends her summers selling her creations on the craft fair circuit. She believes that since she's raised her children, they shouldn't be looking to her for help with *their* children — but when she does have time to spare, it tends to go to Amy and her kids (at least that's how it seems to Robin).

More characters will certainly be added in the course of the writing of the novel — as they are, take the time to write their bios, too, if they have more than walk-on parts.

Meanwhile, take each of the characters you have so far and make a list of ten things that he or she wants. Some of the items on that list will be obvious; you will probably have to do some brainstorming to come up with a complete list of ten, though. Here are lists for Robin and Paul:

Robin wants:

1. to be a good mother
2. to be as famous as Pauline Kael
3. to remodel her house
4. to have a good relationship with her husband (which also means that she wants her husband to pay more attention to her)

5. to make more money writing
6. to find Amy a husband
7. to give Arianna a raise
8. to write a serious book about Francois Truffaut
9. to go to Europe for six months by herself
10. inner peace and spiritual fulfillment

Paul wants:

1. to be a good father
2. to be a good husband (though his concepts of both #1 and #2 are different from Robin's)
3. a particular client to use him as his exclusive stockbroker
4. Robin to do more cooking
5. season tickets to the 49ers
6. Jonathan to grow up to be a Supreme Court justice
7. a bigger office at work
8. to be able to sleep late on weekends
9. the trade deficit reduced
10. a really small sports car, one that might have room for a second person but certainly not a car seat, a diaper bag and a box of rattles along with that second person

These lists will not only deepen your knowledge of the characters, they will also help you start constructing your plot. In fact, we are slipping noiselessly into the place where plot and character meet, because the plot will emerge from what the characters want but can't have.

The building blocks of plot are conflicts. Conflict arises when a character wants something that he or she cannot have because of an obstacle, which is either within the character (internal conflict), exists in the outside environment, or comes in the form of another character wanting the opposite thing (external conflict).

Conflict isn't much fun in life, but it is crucial to fiction. If a character wants something that he *can* have, then the character gets it. Let's say I want a tuna sandwich for lunch. Fine, I make myself one. End of story, and not a very interesting one at that.

But what if I'm out of tuna? Or what if I'm boycotting tuna because tuna-catchers sometimes kill dolphins, too? Or what if I'm highly allergic to tuna? Then I must take some action or make some decision that can potentially lead to other events.

The purpose of the lists I've done for Robin and Paul, that you will do for your characters, is to identify areas of conflict and potential conflict among them. (Note that both Robin and Paul want to be good parents, but since their definitions of what makes a good parent are different, that might actually create conflict.)

Often a character faces both internal and external conflicts. Robin wants to go to Europe by herself, but she would be reluctant to leave her husband and baby, which causes her to be internally conflicted. If she also doesn't have enough money to go, that is an obstacle in the environment, which creates external conflict.

The Main Idea Redux

By now you have collected some pretty serious material. You know a lot more about your characters and their problems than you did starting out. Looking back at our original sketch of *Mommies Don't Cry* at the beginning of this chapter, I see I hadn't really considered a sister as a main character. As I wrote Robin's biography, though, the character of Amy emerged as a potentially funny and revealing counterpart to Robin: the "bad girl" whose life can be an object of longing to the "good girl."

At the same time, as I fleshed out the characters and thought about what they wanted, I lost interest in writing about Robin and Paul remodeling their house. Maybe I'll get back to that, but I won't force myself. A lot of the fun of writing a novel is in discovering it.

I also dropped the character who was to be Robin's best friend, and I made Robin a writer of film reviews rather than novels. I can justify both of those alterations easily enough: Without a best friend to confide in, Robin is more isolated, and more naturally falls prey to Amy's and Arianna's competing needs in exchange for their friendship. And as a film reviewer, Robin will have deadlines that will put more pressure on her than would be on the average novelist.

The truth is, though, that I made neither of these decisions logically. The characters and the story evolve, and then I look back and think about whether I like the way they are evolving.

So go back to your original main idea. Revise and expand it in light of the information you've collected. Trash what's trashable and forge ahead with the new.

Working With a Net

Now for the big plunge. Rough out an outline of the novel itself. When I say rough, I mean *rough*. Think of the outline you do at this point as a safety net rather than a road map. The purpose is to organize the ideas you have and to experiment with putting them together into a series of events that cause one another to happen in sequence.

This is one of the more difficult steps you will take. In a just world, you would now effortlessly summarize the novel in such a way that all that would remain would be to fill in the numbers. Unfortunately, it probably won't work that way. This is your first novel, and you don't know a lot about what works and what doesn't — yet.

Your outline, like the novel itself, is a work-in-progress. For now, it will tell you what you know, and where the sketchier spots in your plot are.

To help you brainstorm your plot, go back to the lists you made of what individual characters want. Ask yourself what obstacles they face to get what they want, and what action they take to overcome those obstacles. The actions will in turn cause other conflicts, which in turn cause other actions, and these actions and conflicts will form the vertebrae of your plot.

Here is a rough outline for *Mommies Don't Cry* (note that the outline of a novel is written in present tense):

Chapter One
Robin has the baby at Children's Hospital (the same place she was born). Her labor is unexpectedly easy, and she falls in love with Jonathan the moment the doctor places him on her chest.

Chapter Two
Robin's and Paul's initial euphoria fade as they spend several sleepless nights trying to figure out what in God's name will make adorable little Jonathan stop crying for ten minutes.

Robin begs her mother, Frances, to come over and help her. Frances does, but then she spends most of the time sitting on the sofa, complaining about a swollen ankle and Robin's father. She keeps reminding Robin that she's already raised three children and doesn't plan to raise Jonathan on Robin's behalf.

Paul is suddenly overloaded at work and spending less time at home. Robin is angry because she suspects his current client load is no coincidence and she says that he could work fewer hours if he wanted.

Chapter Three
Robin interviews baby-sitters who can take care of Jonathan in the morning while she writes her film reviews (after two months, her maternity leave is up).

There could be several short, but hopefully funny, scenes of her interviewing various baby-sitters for the job. They are flaky, inexperienced or even bizarre — maybe one disappears into the bathroom three times during the interview. Finally Robin interviews Arianna, who seems like Mother Teresa compared to the others.

Chapter Four

Jonathan is three months old now and his colic has abated. He gets up once a night, and Robin is still tired, but feeling better than she was. Arianna is showing her a lot about taking care of a baby, and Robin is beginning to feel dependent on her.

Her dependence on Arianna increases when the features editor at the magazine unexpectedly quits and Robin is offered a chance to take over her more demanding job. This is a career opportunity Robin has been waiting for, so she takes it, even though she doesn't want to be away from home more.

Chapter Five

Arianna tells Robin that her former employer has offered Arianna more money and better hours if she'll come back to work for her (Arianna is not thrilled with the extra hours she has taken on since Robin got her more time-consuming job).

Robin asks Paul if they can meet this other offer. He feels they are being blackmailed and refuses.

At the park that weekend, Robin sees the woman Arianna used to work for. The woman is smugly pregnant with her second child, and Robin pointedly ignores her (later she might suspect Arianna or having made up the other offer in an attempt to get more money out of the Deckers).

Robin demands that Paul let her give Arianna a raise and he agrees, but it increases the tension between them.

Chapter Six

One night Paul comes home late, with only a vague explanation, and Robin begins to suspect that he is having an affair. She is particularly leery of a female stockbroker in the office.

Against her better judgment, Robin confides in Arianna, who takes the old world view that "men will be men."

Feeling more vulnerable than ever, Robin picks a fight with Paul the next time he is late. (Maybe it turns out that he's taken up playing poker with the guys just to get some time to himself?)

Chapter Seven

Amy arrives on Friday night, accompanied by her two children, saying that she has an opportunity to go away for a weekend with a man she is certain to marry. Frances had promised to baby-sit Jennie and Toby, but at the last minute Frances decided to travel to Oregon with a carload of pottery to sell at a fair. Robin knows this is typical of Amy, but she agrees to watch the kids.

Amy has never disciplined Jennie or Toby very well and they make a wreck of the house, drawing on newly painted walls and digging up the backyard.

When Paul explodes, Robin feels that she has to defend her niece and nephew to him. The weekend is such a disaster that Paul moves out.

Chapter Eight

Amy returns to pick up Jennie and Toby. She reports that her own weekend was a failure and that remarriage is not in her immediate future. When Robin tells her that Paul has moved out, though, Amy casually blames Robin, whom she says is too much of a nag and a perfectionist.

Arianna's mother falls ill in Greece, and Arianna leaves to visit her for a few weeks.

Robin must take a leave of absence from her job to care for Jonathan. This is the first time in several months that she has acted as a full-time mother and, in spite of the stress she is under, she finds she likes it. She can apply what Arianna has taught her but make up her own rules, too.

Chapter Nine

Paul wants to come back—he misses his family—and Robin wants him back, but on the condition that he go for counseling with her. He agrees.

Arianna returns from Greece. She tells Robin that she is going to bring her mother to the United States and retire from baby-sitting to care for her full-time. Now Robin is happy about the change: She's looking forward to a new relationship with a different baby-sitter in which Robin takes a stronger role.

Amy meets a new man, and this time it looks like it's for real.

Robin decides to give up the job as features editor and continue to write film reviews. She can start working on the serious book she's always wanted to write about Francois Truffaut when she's at home, which will make it easier to spend more time with Jonathan.

Meanwhile, she and Paul plan to take a vacation with Jonathan so that they can all get reacquainted.

What I've written is sketchy for a finished novel, but it's more than enough to get me started and to keep me going for a while. Later, I'll come back to it, make it more detailed, throw out what doesn't work, and refine what does.

You may come up with more, or less, than my outline above. Push yourself to put down as much as you know, *and then a little bit more*. But if there is some plot device you really get stuck on, then just note that down. For example: "Something happens that causes Robin to realize that she's not such a bad mother after all." Or: "I think Robin rushing Jonathan to the hospital is kind of hokey, and a rip-off of that scene in *Kramer vs. Kramer*, but I'll try it."

Whose Story Is It, Anyway?

Now the time has come to choose a point of view. Chapter eight includes a more extensive discussion of this element of writing, which is highly complex (many successful novelists have yet to master it). For now, though, let's ask simply, who is going to tell our story and in what person?

It's likely that the point of view will seem rather obvious to you. To me, it seems natural that since this is Robin's story, she should tell it in the first person.

Many first-time novelists are drawn to the first-person point of view, which means that a character in the novel speaks directly to the reader, describing the action, and referring to himself as "I." This is especially common when one identifies strongly with one's main character.

The chief pitfall of the first-person novel is that one can become a bit close to the material, and some editors criticize these novels as being too self-indulgent. Not every protagonist can be Holden Caulfield. It's sometimes said, in fact, that J.D. Salinger ruined an entire generation of authors by making *Catcher in the Rye* look so easy.

In Anne Lamott's novel *Joe Jones*, a character complains, "It's so weird inside my head." In the third person, we can be outside that character's head, looking in to see the weirdness but not overwhelmed by it.

But consider, too, that the first-person point of view can also be very intimate, creating the sense that the reader is being drawn into the main character's confidence. It's not the only way to write a novel, nor the best way to write all novels, but intuitively, it seems to me the way to tell Robin's story.

The Opening Scene

There are two factors to consider in choosing an opening scene. The first is, where does the real story begin?

Mommies Don't Cry could already be said to be about a lot of things: Robin's relationship with her husband, with her sister, with her baby's nanny, and with Jonathan himself. It's also about her struggle to move on with her career, even though she has a new, frequently noisy priority in her life.

All these relationships and issues arise from the fact that Robin has given birth to Jonathan, so it would seem that is where the story begins — not fifteen years before, when Robin starts Stanford, nor three years before, when Robin first meets Paul.

The second factor to consider is, what is dramatic enough to deserve a scene? It doesn't have to be the birth of a baby, the death of a loved one, or the outbreak of World War III. But neither do we want to hear about an ordinary day in the characters' lives. We want the novel to be the start of something *extra*ordinary.

That's why, as a rule, you want to begin your novel with a scene. Avoid the temptation to lard on a lot of background information about the characters — where they grew up and what they think about the current administration. Instead, let them jump right into their stories and reveal who they are through their actions. Whatever background that's necessary for us to know will simply come up.

Mommies is an easy call, because a birth is inherently dramatic. If the choice doesn't seem so obvious, then ask yourself, "What is the story of the novel about?" and begin there, or just before. *Gone With the Wind* begins the day before the Civil War is declared. Judith Rossner's *August*, the story of an analysis, begins when the patient-heroine arrives for her first session. Scott Turow's *Presumed Innocent* begins the day *after* the murder of Carolyn Polhemus.

Ask yourself, what is the event that starts all the trouble? Because there must be trouble in a novel, or we will have nothing to read about. Franz Kafka's *The Metamorphosis* begins when Gregor Samsa awakens to find himself changed into a giant vermin. That would put a crimp in anyone's day.

Novelists — and not just first-time novelists — have a tendency to begin their novels too early. They hesitate to bring out their big guns right away; they fear that they will have nothing to write after a dramatic opening.

The more you write, the more you will have to write. Give the reader a dramatic opening and let that inspire the next scene. To put it another way: Bring out your big guns, then bring out *bigger* guns.

You know what I'm going to say, but I'll say it anyway: The opening scene you write doesn't have to be the opening scene you end up with. You can always change it later. (There.)

Here's a possible opening for our own, excuse the expression, embryonic novel:

> Looking back, I guess I went into labor about nine in the morning. But in the Lamaze classes, they tell us not to pay too much attention to the occasional cramp; wait until the pains get serious before you decide to come to the hospital.
>
> By the time I had a serious contraction, it was after noon and I was buying typing paper at the office supply store. I gripped the counter and let out a howl.
>
> "Are you all right?" the cashier asked. He was only about eighteen, and trying to grow a beard that so far looked like sandpaper.
>
> *Yes*, I thought, *I always scream like this when I'm feeling fine.* "Can I use your phone?" I asked as soon as I could catch my breath.
>
> "We don't have a pay phone," the cashier smirked, looking at the phone next to the cash register.
>
> "I'd be happy to give you twenty cents," I said, "but unless you want to go in the back room and start boiling some water, you should probably let me use your phone."

What follows your opening scene may occur to you naturally. If it doesn't, this is where your outline will help you.

You've gotten some momentum going. Don't lose it. Meanwhile — guess what? You got that novel started!

TO GET THAT NOVEL STARTED

Proceed from basic idea to character studies to outline to opening scene.

CHAPTER SEVEN

Begin the Beginning

Words to Live (or Die) By

In the preceding chapter, we rather casually began our novel. No sweat, right? I was hoping to sneak it past you.

But I realize that the complicated issue of beginnings deserves a little more time than that.

Let's say you've accumulated volumes of background material, from interviews with the minor characters to extended notes about the history of the cities in which they were born.

Still, on the long, dark road that is a novel, you come to a lot of spooky junctions, and this is one. Because now you are ready to write that first sentence. When you do, you are no longer doing homework—you're writing the novel.

Most of the wannabes who are going to bail out do it right here. They find a brightly lit truck stop with the other wannabes, drink coffee all night, and talk about how tough it is to have an artistic temperament.

It's understandable. Consider the intimidating history:

- "Call me Ishmael."
- "It was the best of times, it was the worst of times."
- "Scarlett O'Hara was not beautiful. . . ."
- "Garp's mother, Jenny Fields, was arrested in Boston in 1942 for wounding a man in a movie theater."
- "All happy families are alike; each unhappy family is unhappy in its own particular way."

You, the first-time novelist and book lover, naturally wish to join this celebrated canon, and that is a noble ambition.

But that also may mean that you tell yourself, if I can't write that perfect beginning, how the heck am I going to survive the next 400 pages?

Still, when I said that this was a favorite permanent truck stop for wannabes, I lied (though it's the first time, I swear). A lot of writers carry around a dynamite opening sentence for years, and one day they write it down, but then they can't come up with a *second* sentence that quite matches the first for depth and impact. After a couple of hours of sweating, slam go the brakes, and it's truck stop city.

If the first sentence is holding you up, try this: Draw a line across the top of the page, or type out about sixty Xs (occasionally breaking the series by hitting the space bar), put a period at the end, and then begin your novel with sentence #2.

If you already have a lovely, eye-catching first sentence, a sentence so clever that it will serve as an epigraph for generations of novels to come, write it down, but finish the paragraph with the same lines or Xs if necessary. Don't forget to throw in a few commas and semicolons.

Writers Just Want to Have Fun

Of course you do have to write that first sentence eventually, and maybe you'll just feel better if it's written now. Okay.

As every four-year-old knows (but adult writers tend to forget), it's fun to play. So here are some ideas for tinkering around with that first sentence, until you come up with one you love:

1. Create a mood.

"It was a brand new day, a day that had never been before, and Robin awoke feeling hopeful."

2. Go ahead and shock us.

"There was a lot of blood, and Robin thought she was dying."

3. Foreshadow a major event in the story or even tell us the end.

"A year later, when my husband and I were talking about divorce, we both fondly remembered the birth of our first child."

Here's how Gabriel Garcia Marquez did it in his novel, *A Hundred Years of Solitude*:

"Many years later, as he faced the firing squad, Colonel Aureliano Buendia was to remember that distant afternoon when his father took him to discover ice."

4. State the theme of the book.

The trap you can fall into here is sounding a bit preachy; if you're going to deliver a message, see if you can avoid the obvious, or at least phrase it in some more personal, original way. You can start with:

"Motherhood is much harder than anyone expects, but also more worthwhile."

But this is a little better:

"Being a mommy was both a job and an adventure."

5. Challenge yourself to reveal as much as possible about the main character.

"For a small woman without much in the way of hips, for a college-educated woman without much in the way of childbirth experience, and for a woman married only a short time without much in the way of experience with men (granted, she was thirty-five), Robin Sovicki-Decker did not fare badly in the delivery room."

A clunker, you say? Maybe, but consider the opening sentence of John Barth's cult classic, *The Sot-Weed Factor*:

> In the last years of the Seventeenth Century there was to be found among the fops and fools of the London coffee-houses one rangy, gangling flitch called Ebenezer Cooke, more ambitious than talented, yet more talented than prudent, who like his friends-in-folly, all of whom were supposed to be educating at Oxford or Cambridge, had found the sound of Mother English more fun to game with than her sense to labor over, and so rather than applying himself to the pains of scholarship, had learned the knack of versifying, and ground out quires of couplets after the fashion of the day, afroth with *Joves* and *Jupiters*, aclang with jarring rhymes, and string-taut with similes stretched to the breaking point.

The opening of *The Sot-Weed Factor* reveals much about its hero, while it establishes the setting of the novel. But it also shows how a dedicated writer can make music out of words.

So push yourself, experiment—in fooling around lies the opportunity for true brilliance. Don't let your own impatience to become famous distract you from the actual business of writing, which is learning to become a writer.

Of course, you don't want to start with a funny or raunchy first sentence, no matter how much a grabber it is, if the rest of the book is going to be a domestic drama without much comedy or sex.

However you start, *you can change it later*. (There, I've said it yet again.) The opening sentence of *Anna Karenina* (I noted it earlier, "*All happy families are alike . . .*") is often quoted, but the real story begins with the second sentence, "Everything was in confusion in the Oblonsky household," and, if I may be so bold as to comment upon *Anna Karenina*, the book has to rise or fall on the few hundred thousand words that follow. If this be blasphemy, make the most of it.

The Novelist's Curse (Another One)

Let's take a closer look at the process of choosing the opening scene.

Our imaginary novel, *Mommies*, really does present us with a good opportunity in the birth of Robin's baby. But that still leaves us a lot of leeway. Do I start when Robin feels her first twinge, or do I skip ahead to when the doctor tells Robin to start pushing?

A myriad of choices is the novelist's curse.

Begin where it feels right. Begin where you want.

If you want a more specific rule than that, then begin at the most dramatic moment you can find. Is there anything about Robin's early labor that we really need to know? If not, then let her push that baby out into the world. Begin with her screaming, and Paul shouting, "It's a boy!" — or back up just a little bit and have the doctor wondering aloud whether they need to do a C-section.

Novels can be about conspiracies to assassinate world leaders, or scullery maids who marry princes. But they don't have to be: Our quieter lives can just as easily be the raw material for dramatic fiction. The problem is that first-time novelists too often miss the dramatic moments within those ordinary lives — the confrontations, the decisions, the risks.

Not-So-Beautiful Dreamers

James N. Frey has said, "Use a dream, lose a reader."

I generally prefer to suggest "do's" rather than "don'ts," and it really is true that there are no absolute rules. *However*: Dreams by their nature are abstract and symbolic. We don't yet know what the reality of the novel is and here is the author presenting us with a gloss on that reality.

Imagine this was the first scene of *Mommies*:

> Dark. A tunnel. A light. Then a train going through the tunnel. The priestess came down the steps of the temple, and somehow her mother was there, too.
>
> The light and shadow were still alternating. A dog barked.

She knew she should sing along with him, but she needed more time.

Robin awoke in a sweat.

As readers, our minds quickly dismiss the false reality, and grab onto the "real" reality—meanwhile feeling mildly ripped off, because we've already been fooled, even for a few sentences, about what's actually going on in the novel.

If you need further convincing that dreams are not the way to go, recall the way you felt the last time that strange guy at work told you what he dreamt the night before.

Begin After the Beginning

The pressure's really on in the beginning. You know from your own reading that if you're not interested after a few pages, you put the book down. You know, too, that once you've read up to page 100 or so, you'll cut the same author a little slack.

But you have to write those first 100 pages first, right? All the while the Beast is growling at you, "What kind of foul-smelling, fly-attracting abomination in the eyes of the Lord is *this*?

Shh! Don't tell! I have a trick to play on the Beast: *Forget the beginning.*

That's right! Never mind the beginning at all!

Let's say that I've spent a month or more fooling around with the opening scene of *Mommies*. By now, I feel like I'm in labor myself. Nothing I've come up with—setting, opening sentence, lines of dialogue—feels right.

Or, worse, I've spent a month in a state of near paralysis, unable to press a single key of my computer.

So I look back at my outline, and start in the middle of the book. If possible, I will start with a scene that is dramatic and pivotal. (A pivotal scene is one that changes the relationships of the characters; an example of a pivotal scene would be one in which Jonathan's nanny, Arianna, quits, or Paul and Robin fight and he moves out.)

Later I can go back and write those first 100 pages. Meanwhile, it's as if, instead of getting out at that truck stop, I had someone fly by in a helicopter, pick me up and drop me off a few miles closer to my destination.

You may even discover that what you thought was the middle of the novel actually *is* the beginning (recall that I said that novelists tend to begin their novels too early). If that is the case, then your initial resistance will have worked to your advantage.

Begin Before the Beginning

You can also cross out the words "Chapter One" and scrawl "Prologue" across the top of the page. Tell yourself that since no one reads prologues anyway it doesn't matter what you write.

Seriously, a true prologue has an honored place in fiction, and may actually be just where you want to begin.

"Prologue" comes from Greek, and means "before the discourse." Technically, the prologue is separate from the main action of the novel, and may deal with minor characters, or even characters we might not see again, although the information contained in a prologue should be just as germane as anything else.

Prologues as a rule function in one or more of the following ways:

1. As a framing device.

Imagine a group of Boy and Girl Scouts gathered around a campfire to hear ghost stories. The scoutmaster promises to tell the scariest story of all. Thus begins a horror novel, in the scoutmaster's voice.

Such a framing device (in which a novel is a story-within-a-story) usually presumes an epilogue as well as a prologue, in which some effect on the listeners is made apparent, which adds another dimension to the novel.

2. As a flash-forward.

These are like the previews that a television drama sometimes shows before the credits. For example, your prologue might show a race car driver hurtling toward the finish line, wondering if, in the next few moments, he's going to win a million dollars, or his wheels are going to fall off and he's going to die.

The paradox of suspense is that the more you know, the more you want to know. If we know this kind of dramatic scene is coming, that will heighten our interest in the novel when we meet the race care driver in chapter one. (The same is true in the earlier examples of opening sentences that "give away" a later event of the novel, thus intriguing us to read that novel.)

3. As a flashback.

In this case, the flashback is to a seminal event, that is, something that occurred before the main action of the novel (probably well before), but which is responsible for the main action. Example: Let's change our overall conception of *Mommies*, and say that it's about Paul and Robin raising a child with a disability. The book takes place when Jonathan, the son, is in junior high, but I might decide to begin with a prologue that describes his birth, and how Robin and Paul discover that something has gone wrong.

4. To establish the milieu of the book.

Let's say that the setting of your novel is particularly important. You might choose to include a prologue that highlights what will actually be the backdrop of the novel, before the main characters come onstage.

As with any type of prologue, this is best dramatized. Tom Wolfe did an excellent job of this in *Bonfire of the Vanities*: The mayor of New York is giving a speech in Harlem, which erupts into a riot from which the mayor must flee.

The mayor is a minor character in the novel as a whole, but the prologue establishes the issue of contemporary racial tension in New York as the backdrop for the personal drama of the protagonist, Sherman McCoy.

The First Shall Be the Last

A friend of mine who writes short stories likes to write the final scene of the story first. That gives him something to aim toward, and the confidence that he won't write himself into a corner.

I think this is a fine idea. Try it, if it sounds like a fine idea to you, too. Writing the end is going to give you ideas about the beginning. This is true of writing any part of the novel, but especially the end, because in that final scene, more than any other, many of the notes you have struck earlier will be sounded again.

Let's say I write the final scene of *Mommies*. Robin and Paul are reconciling. Robin hugs him and notices the reassuring scent of his after-shave. That gives me the idea that in the opening scene, as they are driving to the hospital, that Robin can notice the same after-shave—but here, when she's in early labor and very nervous, the odor makes her nauseous.

I must caution you, though, if you write the end first, not to fall into the trap of thinking that this is a shorter, quicker way to write. Maybe that final scene will remain unchanged, and you can just add it to the other pages when you complete the rest of the draft of your novel, but that's not very likely, if only because you will be a much better writer by then, and you'll want to make the final scene better, too.

Blissful Ignorance, or How Much of the Story Do You Need to Know?

This leads us to another frequently asked question on the novel-writing circuit. How much of the story do you need to know before you begin?

Here is John Irving on the matter:

> Know the story—as much of the story as you can possibly know, if not the whole story—before you commit yourself to the first paragraph. Know the story—the whole story if possible—before you fall in love with your first *sentence*, not to mention your first chapter. If you don't know the story before you begin the story, what kind of storyteller are you? Just an ordinary kind, just a mediocre kind—making it up as you go along, like a common liar.

Other writers, like Flannery O'Connor, talk about discovering a novel as they write it. Leonard Bishop used to exhort his students not to make outlines, *any* outlines. For some reason, outlines seemed to annoy him.

Here are my own, and rather strong feelings on the matter: I said in chapter one that thinking—gestating—can only take you so far. At some point, preferably sooner rather than later, you have to start putting words on paper.

This is when the exercises I described in the preceding chapter are not only valuable; they're crucial. You can get to know your characters and experiment with your plot in the loosest environment.

Or you can start off with writing text if you want—that's fine, too. But you'll almost certainly end up going back to do those biographies, monologues, and lists of what people want a little bit later, when you feel your characters floundering on the page.

Now, I've always felt a little uncomfortable when writers talked of their creations taking over. "Kari just refused to do what I wanted her to do!" an author pouted to me once. "That's a pity," I clucked, but what I wanted to say was, *Uh, you do realize, don't you, that Kari does not actually exist?*

And yet, at the risk of copping one of those same artistic attitudes, I do believe that it is in the actual writing of the book that the characters assume more lifelike proportions. When you write scenes and dialogue, and move your characters through their fictional world, the most concrete and original ideas for the story will come to you. Although Kari the dental hygienist does not actually exist, you can't entirely anticipate what story lines will work for her character until you get her into this fictional world.

Let's look at it another way. Before you get an idea for a novel, you don't know *any*thing about it. Then one day you get an idea. If you keep writing (and thinking) about that idea long enough, eventually you end up with a novel, at which point you know *every*thing about it.

The finished product that is your novel will reflect that process. Of course, you don't write the book straight through and leave the beginning in its original state. You go back to the beginning many times, and structure it so that it prepares us for what you finally know is to follow. I didn't say writing a novel was easy.

A novel, in fact, is a big messy jigsaw puzzle, and you can't get all the teeny tiny parts together in perfect order. When you finally put that last piece in, though, what you have is a seamless picture that doesn't look as though it was ever in a zillion pieces.

This is in perfect agreement with Irving's advice. Notice that he said you need to know the whole story before you "*commit* to the first paragraph" or "*fall in love* with" the first sentence (italics mine). When you put the final pieces in, when you *do* know the entire story, then you can commit and fall in love, not necessarily in that order.

Now, this does not mean you should write 500 pages without any idea of where you're going, cheerfully deluding yourself that the muse will provide. You may find that you need to have an alien spaceship take all your characters away to Uranus to clean up the debris of your novel.

Start with the basic idea, do some background exercises, and then shape that basic idea into the best outline you can. As you learn more about the book, refine the outline. Eventually you and your story will know each other, and then you can tell it to the world.

TO GET THAT NOVEL STARTED

Begin at the beginning. If you don't know what the beginning is, then begin before the beginning or begin in the middle or at the end.

CHAPTER EIGHT

What It Looks Like When You're Finished

Novel Heaven

This chapter provides you with an overview of the elements of a well-written novel. This is the model that you will be swimming toward as you write.

The variations of the form of a novel are endless. Use this overview for further inspiration, that is, for ways of experimenting with your idea or rekindling your interest. It can only help you to know the rules before you break them; and the greater your mastery of the rules, the more skillfully you can do just that.

But, on those days when you feel you should quit because you'll never master the rules, then forget the rules and write anyway.

Characters and Their Different Shapes

Character is the core of fiction. The most intricate plot exists so that we will care about what happens to the people involved; the finest-crafted prose exists so that we know how people feel. The novel itself can't exist without characters, although those "characters" might be animals, gods, or forces of nature that stand in for people.

We have discussed how getting to know your characters yourself is the first, best way of making them live on the page. Your brain is the hard disk, into which you store as much information and understanding of a particular person as possible. Then, when a situation arises, you know immediately what that person would do. For example, you probably know, long before you tell her, exactly how your wife will react when she finds out what you spent on a new suit. Even if she reacts "out of character," and says a simple, "That's nice, dear," you understand why—she had a good day, or she's making an honest attempt to be less critical.

The satisfaction of knowing people (and loving them in spite of their flaws), the frustration of another person's self-satisfaction, and the recognition of our own human limitations are some of the motives behind our desire to create passionate, fully realized characters.

Before we get too heavy, though, let's make the distinction between round and flat characters, first made by E.M. Forster in *Aspects of the Novel.*

The central characters in a novel are round. Whether or not the author goes into their heads to take their point of view, we are able to perceive them to some extent from the inside; we have some idea of how they tick. They have dominant, striking personality traits, just like real people, but also like real people, they are multi-dimensional, even contradictory. A young man's fear contains his potential for courage; an aging woman's acceptance of death contains her nostalgia for her youth.

The round characters must change in the course of a novel and ideally that change will go to the very heart of their personalities (which will have helped to create the story that changed them). Robin Sovicki, as the main character of *Mommies Don't Cry*, is a round character. One of her main problems is her insecurity—that's what got her into the mess she's in—so we will want to see her resolve that problem, which means that ultimately she must change. But that change will be from "the potential to the actual," as Leon Surmelian says in *Techniques of Fiction Writing.* We will know from early on that she has the potential to be a firm, confident mother; whether she is able to actualize that potential will create suspense in the novel, although to be truly suspenseful, we must see that question acted out somehow, not just debated over in the character's or the author's mind.

Other examples: The protagonist of Tom Wolfe's *The Bonfire of the Vanities* is the hopelessly arrogant Sherman McCoy. In his arrogance, he believes that he will always be rich, that he deserves to be rich, and that a rich aristocrat such as himself should have a beautiful mistress. We want to see him humbled, and we do: He gets lost in the Bronx, a foreign country to a resident of Manhattan's Upper East Side, and there he's involved in an accident. The accident causes his life to unravel until he's left poor and alone, without money, wife or mistress. The change in this round character undergoes cuts to his core.

In *A Tale of Two Cities*, Sydney Carton is a self-pitying drunkard and failed barrister who nevertheless inspires our affection because of his love for Lucy Manette. At the end of the novel he gives his life so that Lucy and her husband can escape France's reign of terror. Sydney is round: his capacity for such a gesture was always there, but it lies dormant until circumstance draws it out.

Flat characters live more in the background of a novel. They may create obstacles for the main characters (which is the same as saying that they may function to further the plot), but we don't follow their personal psychic journey. They don't change; they are the same at the end as they are at the beginning. Flat characters may also appear for a short time, then disappear out of the novel; we don't need to know their ultimate destinies.

Flat characters give you an opportunity to carve up your subject with a sharper instrument. We said that in chapter three of *Mommies* there would be a series of short scenes in which Robin interviews baby-sitters who are flaky and even bizarre. These baby-sitters are flat; their purpose is to show us what Robin faces in choosing someone to take care of her baby, to dramatize the modern dilemma of a woman who wants both career and motherhood.

These women (let's assume they are all women) will exhibit more extremes of behavior than similar women would in life. (Real life can be mundane. Fiction should never be.) Besides disappearing into the bathroom three times during the interview, maybe one of the applicants arrives with a big, slobbering dog that she insists accompany her everywhere. Maybe another gives voice to some occult philosophies, and a third doesn't show up at all.

Thus you can "tag" flat characters, focusing on one aspect of their personalities in any way that serves your purposes. Suppose Jonathan's pediatrician is another flat character in *Mommies*. His tag could be his alarmist style. In the hospital, he solemnly warns Robin, "If the baby looks yellow, he has JAUNDICE. Call me immediately! Jaundice can be fatal!"

This serves our purpose in that Robin is a worrier, and though she'd probably think of things to worry about on her own, the doctor will really be able to make her sweat. He might spark her to make rash decisions or encourage her to rush Jonathan to the emergency room unnecessarily.

While most real-life doctors, besides warning their patients of possible disasters, also demonstrate compassion, impatience, expertise, endurance, insight and/or indifference at various times, it is both useful and legitimate to have flat characters who repeatedly exhibit one quality.

A lot of humor can arise from the predictability of a character as well. When Robin picks up the phone to call the doctor because Jonathan has a fever, we know he's going to raise the spectre of spinal meningitis, and we know that the fretful Robin is going to focus on that suggestion. She and the pediatrician are well matched.

As a rule, the important characters in your novel will be round. Robin will obviously be a round character, as will Paul, Arianna and Amy, with whom she has her most pivotal adult relationships. That is not to say that there won't be a predictable dimension to the round characters. With Robin's sister Amy, for example, there will be little doubt in the reader's mind that each promising romance she embarks upon will end in disappointment. But as a round character, Amy not only can change, she can change in crucial ways. At the end, she'll get her man (although for that to be believable, we must know enough about her insides to understand how she has struggled with and triumphed over inner obstacles).

Round characters are no better than flat characters. A novel needs both: round characters with whom the reader identifies, and flat characters to provide a social backdrop and to help move the story forward. These flat characters can more easily serve as mouthpieces for the author, expressing philosophic points of view that would sound stilted coming from main characters. They should never be stereotypes, but they can definitely be, not only predictable, but idiosyncratic and eccentric. (Charles Dickens was particularly adept at creating memorable flat characters, who are nowadays more famous than his round, but sometimes a bit bland, central characters.)

Sometimes an author will people a comic novel entirely with flat characters (John Kennedy Toole did this quite hysterically in *A Confederacy of Dunces*). What this type of book needs is a rollicking, improbable story made probable by the author's wit and inventiveness. At the bottom of the story, too, must lie a solid foundation of insight into society's foibles. This social dimension is what fills the vacuum created by the absence of the rounded hero or heroine.

The Main Character, or the Burden of Being the Star

One of the most common pitfalls that await the first-time novelist is the tendency to make main characters too passive, too much the victim. That can happen because the author identifies most strongly with his main character, and wishes, naturally, for the reader to like this character. The author is then fearful of having the character do anything to lose this affection. The trouble is, that as soon as anybody does anything, there is the potential for alienating *some*body, so pretty soon the poor main character is boxed in, with a very limited range of options.

We can already see that as a trap Robin could fall into. We've described her as buffeted about, under pressure from a lot of different directions. A character *should* be under pressure, but she must also be able to rise to the challenges life throws at her, and rise to those challenges *now*, not a few chapters from now. As James N. Frey puts it in *How to Write a Damn Good Novel*, "The protagonist of a dramatic novel should always be determined, well-motivated, willful."

One way to combat the tendency to make main characters too passive is to find what they care about most passionately, what they are willing to go to the mats for. Your main character must have a goal that he will do anything to achieve.

In Robin's case it would be the well-being of her baby. She is willing to fight her husband and family, willing to risk her job, willing to drive through a hurricane to buy formula.

It may be in the opening scene, when Jonathan is born, that Robin first discovers her new goal in life: to be a good mother. The rest of the novel is her struggle to achieve that, and some of that struggle will be within herself. That's fine, since it's something she cares about so deeply. But again, beware of the trap of letting a character's conflict remain too internal, and therefore lying undramatized. Instead, let the environment provide obstacles that will force the characters to confront *in the outside world* representations of the demons they face within.

Another way to combat the tendency of main characters to become dull is simply to leap in and take some chances with letting them loose on the page. Go ahead and let her express a few of those less-than-noble thoughts you've had. Let her tell a lie, or walk by a beggar without giving him money. Only certain genres of novels demand a main character of always-heroic proportions. Besides, unless your protagonist is the Messiah, he or she must have *some* faults.

At the same time, a sympathetic main character is an advantage in a novel. It is naturally easier for readers to care about a person they can like. There are many exceptions to the sympathetic-main-character rule: Scarlett O'Hara is a famous one. To the extent that your characters are *not* likable, though, they have to be that much more interesting/amusing/articulate to overcome the reader's resistance to them.

How do you make your characters likable? Simply attributing

"nice" traits to them may only make them dull, unbelievable or even buffoonish. Think of a man who constantly gives in to his girlfriend's demands, or a teenage girl who loans all her clothes to her friends so that they can wear them on their dates.

We will actually be more sympathetic with a character who is struggling with his or her baser nature. Consider: Amy appears on Robin's doorstep, with her children in tow, wanting Robin to take them for the weekend. Robin's got a lot going on: a new job, a fussy infant, a moody husband, and a baby-sitter glued to the Home Shopping Club. Still, if she refuses, she's not very likable. Trouble is, if she immediately agrees, she seems like a pushover.

A third alternative is to have Robin think at first, *no way in heck*, but then to show how she relents as she puts herself in her younger sister's place. Amy has two kids and plenty of money troubles, but this weekend she at least has the chance to get away from it all. Robin realizes — eventually — that she can find the resources within herself to help her sister out.

There is a French saying, "To understand all is to forgive all." So even if your main character is a cheapskate who won't give his daughter money to buy a dress for her prom, if you render fully for us the panic he feels at the idea of parting with money — his fear of not making the mortgage, of being out on the street — we will sympathize with his actions.

Dialogue

When you're reading a long passage of description, even a well-written one, you may find yourself cheating a little bit: Your eyes drift down to the end of the paragraph to see if there's any dialogue coming to break the monotony. And if you do find some lively dialogue there at the bottom of that paragraph, chances are you will just keep on reading, rather than go back through that dense passage.

Dialogue not only draws us immediately into the action, it's one of the most concise ways to reveal character. A person's education, ethnic background, current emotional state, profession and ulterior motives can all be dramatized in that person's use of slang, euphemisms, four-letter words, jargon, or highfalutin Latin expressions.

Consider the following examples of dialogue:

- "Dear Miss Havisham," said Miss Sarah Pocket. "How well you look!"

- "Look," I said, "you'd better put that damn blade away and get your head straight."
- "Sunny side? Do that be a remark from our Stick Bride or how she like her eggs, which? Fast."

We know a lot about the above speakers just from their speech, and when these lines of dialogue are part of whole conversations, resting firmly on a bed of gestures, we get to know even more.

In the perfect novel, each character speaks in a way that not only reflects her background but is uniquely hers. How might Robin speak? Amy? Paul? Arianna? (Jonathan will be easy because there are only so many ways you can write, "Da-da.")

Robin, Amy and Paul are all from northern California, but that's not as homogenous a tribe as you might think. I could give Amy a touch of the Valley Girl, sprinkling her speech with "likes" and "you knows," while Paul, the stockbroker, uses a businessman's jargon.

Since Arianna was born in Greece, she would speak English with an accent. But if I spell out each idiosyncrasy in her pronunciations, it will be tedious for the reader and may seem condescending on the author's part, as well. Instead, I can indicate that accent by altering the syntax of her sentences ("I was tired to make dinner," Arianna said). I can also translate some Greek expressions ("She put both his feet in one shoe,") or try to find some exclamation she uses frequently ("I thanked God!").

This last device, of associating a character with certain repeated expressions, is just that—a device. But you can use it, up to a point, to flag characters for the reader. You know those annoying verbal tics that your dear ones have? Lapses of grammar, or fifty-cent words he uses incorrectly? (" 'Penultimate' does not mean 'the absolute ultimate'!" you may have screamed on more than one occasion.) Use 'em all.

Some novelists feel very comfortable writing dialogue, which they seem to have a natural ear for, while others are so intimidated that they'd turn all their characters into mutes if they could get away with it. How to work on dialogue, then?

One of the best ways is the same as any other aspect of writing: Put it down, put it aside, then go back and rewrite it.

The other best way is to start listening.

Now that you're a novelist, you have permission to sit in cafes or on park benches and eavesdrop on other people's conversations. You're not being nosy, you're doing research.

What you will probably discover, though, is the same thing you may have noticed if you've ever read a transcript of a court proceeding or a therapy session: The way people actually talk is boring. They repeat themselves, they grope for words, they grunt instead of being specific. Your job is to capture those true-to-life rhythms and strategies, while compressing the number of words, to convey more concisely their meaning and purpose.

Here again, your family and close friends are a particularly good resource for learning to write dialogue, in part because you have had the opportunity to talk to them over months and years, and in part because your interactions have ranged from "What movie do you want to see?" to "You've disappointed me all my life."

Besides having access to a certain vocabulary, each of us has characteristic ways of communicating verbally. My grandmother liked to argue by repeating her original thesis over and over again, while simply ignoring what the other person had to say. My father, an excellent teacher and lawyer, also has just a slight tendency to fall into Socratic questioning, as in, "Now, Donna, what do *you* think is the difference between an A term paper and a B term paper?"

As for myself, I've been told by more than one exasperated listener that I too often digress onto completely different subjects right in the middle of my sentences. I'd give Robin the same habit but I'm afraid it might get awfully annoying. What I would like to do is make her funny. She always has a dry observation or self-deprecating remark at the ready.

Good dialogue, like good everything else in your novel, will further the story. It's also usually more interesting, for example, to listen to a captain describing a dangerous mission to his men, than it is to read a long block of narration describing how the men were told about the mission. The former is immediate and compelling; the latter distances us from the action.

In your own mission to further the story in dialogue, however, you must avoid expository dialogue, or what I like to call the Soap Opera Trap. In soap operas (sorry—I mean daytime dramas), the writers must allow for the poor slobs who need to go to school or to work occasionally and can't watch every day. Therefore they must constantly find ways of updating the viewers about the story. Millicent says to Angelique: "They're releasing our brother Robert from prison today, after serving just two years of his sentence for armed robbery."

In real-life, people don't tell each other things they already know. Instead, narrate that information thusly:

> "I'm going to pick up Robert," Millicent said.
>
> Angelique, her sister, did not reply for a moment. Robert was their brother, and he was being released from prison that day, after serving just two years of his ten-year sentence for armed robbery.
>
> "Oh, my God," Angelique said at last.

Dribbling background in this way, through the dialogue, keeps us reading present-time action and removes the temptation to the reader to skip down to the end of a paragraph.

The other extreme, which you must also avoid, is talking heads: long passages of clever, or sometimes not-so-clever, dialogue in which there are so few references to the environment that we lose track of who is speaking. Instead, combine your dialogue with body language and props, to underscore what the characters are saying.

Of course, sometimes everything the characters say is meant to cover over what they cannot say. Henry James was a master at having characters hint at all sorts of shocking behavior, without ever uttering an improper word. A hundred or so years later, we're allowed to utter more of those improper words; but we're also still reading Henry James.

Overall Structure

As a general rule, a novel is more than 50,000 words (a short story is fewer than 30,000, and a novella is 30,000 to 50,000 words). More important than length, though, is the structure; that is, the way the events relate to one another.

In a short story, one thing happens to one person, and everything else in the story exists to support that one event (which leads to an insight that causes the character to change, if only in this added knowledge). A novel, however, is more than a long short story, and more than a series of short stories strung together, that just happen to have the same characters. It is much broader is scope, and yet no less tightly structured.

The first element you must put in place is causation. Each event must cause the one that follows. But each event as it occurs also builds on the one before, ups the stakes, puts more pressure on the characters.

Then, at the end of the novel, these events will be shown to have had a purpose, leading us to a particular conclusion about the world you have created. James N. Frey calls this the "premise" of your novel, a term earlier used by Lajos Egri in *The Art of Dramatic Writing* to apply to stage plays.

The premise of your novel is the point of it. It is similar to the "moral" or the "theme," but a premise needn't be profound (although it's likely to be, simply because it will be something that you care a lot about). The premise arises from the unity you have imposed on the events you have created.

To illustrate with *Mommies Don't Cry*: Robin gives birth to a child. Her new responsibilities are daunting at first, and she has trouble fulfilling them as she would like. But eventually she triumphs over the challenges she faces. The premise is: *Motherhood makes you a stronger person.*

Is that always true? Of course not. But it is true for this novel, and it is the point of it. Therefore, it is the premise. If I want, I can write another novel about a woman who lives in the suburbs, drives a station wagon to PTA meetings, and gets up at 5 A.M. to do her son's paper route. She's dutiful, but she hates all of it. One day she leaves her family to find fame and fortune as a country-western singer. When she returns to see her children a year later, she discovers that they are much happier with their homebody father and his new wife than they were with her, their restless, dissatisfied mom. The premise of this novel would be: *Freedom is more important than motherhood.*

Have you ever been reading a novel, and about halfway through you find yourself thinking, "What's the point?" The novel probably had an ill-defined premise. What a premise does is give your novel a focus. That is why, although many things happen in a novel, it has *one premise*. If you try to have more than one premise, your novel will have to go off in more than one direction, trying to prove them both.

You may not know what "the point" of your novel is when you start to write it, and that's fine. But it's good to articulate your premise for yourself when you can. The end of the first draft is a good time: By then you have allowed yourself to do your share of experimenting and discovering, and it's time to start making some decisions as to what the book really is about.

The value of knowing your premise lies in being able to use it to test whether or not a particular episode belongs in your novel. Now that we know our premise for *Mommies*, we can go back and ask about each event, Does this lead us to our conclusion?

Suppose I write what I think is a wonderfully funny, quirky

scene in which Robin's Aunt Estelle comes to visit from Los Angeles. Robin's aunt is an eccentric collector who likes to scrounge around garage sales looking for priceless antiques. Imagine the high jinks when Aunt Estelle finds what she's convinced is an original copy of the Magna Carta!

But if you ask, "What has that got to do with the premise, that motherhood makes you a stronger person?" then I must answer, not darn much, not at first glance, anyway. Therefore, the scene probably doesn't belong in the novel.

As I've said, there are no shortcuts. Getting started is the hardest part of writing a novel, but rewriting is the longer part.

Be willing to write a scene such as the one with Aunt Estelle as part of the first draft, to see where it leads. Be willing to cut it when it doesn't lead anywhere and when, in retrospect, it doesn't serve to prove your premise.

Pace

Pace refers to the rhythm of the action. You've got to keep the beat: not too fast, not too slow. By far the more common problem that authors have is the latter, although throwing car races, kidnappings, hydrogen bombs and garbage strikes at us on every page without giving us time to assess the impact of these events, isn't a good idea, either.

A novel often begins with some sort of narrative hook—a big bang, if you will—and then slows somewhat. As the novel progresses, the pace gradually accelerates again until, at the end, everything gets tied up in a big finale.

Look at popular movies for examples of this. *Star Wars* begins with the boarding of Princess Leia's ship by the Empire. This is a cinematic hook. After Leia is captured and her 'droids escape, the scene switches to a desolate planet and the action slows (comparatively speaking) as the fate of the 'droids who crash there unfolds.

Star Wars is a fast-paced film throughout, but the pace gets even quicker as the action progresses, through a series of dramatic rescues and close calls, until the last battle scene, which is the big finale.

How might this apply to our novel? *Mommies Don't Cry* will not be another *Star Wars*. But even in a more reflective work of fiction, the same rules of pace apply.

A narrative hook implies something stronger than simply choosing the scene where the story begins. In *Mommies*, it might be the difference between mellowly describing the color of a newborn's skin and having medical personnel screaming things like "Code Blue!" as Robin is rushed on a gurney through swinging doors with all the urgency of the opening of the old "Ben Casey" show.

When in doubt, err on the side of the swinging doors with the following limitation: Don't tack on a dramatic, exciting scene that has little or nothing to do with the story that follows. I once read a manuscript that began with a man being knifed in an alley. End of knife, end of alley—it turned out the murdered man was the main character's uncle, who the main character didn't even like. The sole point of the uncle's death was to give the main character a reason to be in a bad mood that day.

The purpose of a narrative hook is to give us a chance to get to know the characters painlessly, in the sense that we're not aware of getting to know them, we're just aware of wondering what will happen.

What complications will Robin face as she goes into labor? Will the baby be a girl or a boy? Will Paul faint in the delivery room? These questions and more, as the saying goes, should keep us in adequate suspense until we get involved with the characters as individuals.

Also, since we first meet Robin and Paul at a time of high stress and excitement, they will be forced to reveal the best and worst of themselves, which is a good way to get to know who people are.

After the author has gotten our attention, the action of the novel will be somewhat slower, for example, during the first months of the baby's life, as Robin and Paul discover what it really is like not to have time to take a shower or to have to drag themselves off to work after being up half the night.

Gradually the pace will accelerate: first, as Robin finds herself alienated from Paul and dependent upon Arianna, and then when the pressures increase at work as well. During the final third of the novel the relationships will reach a crisis point, as Robin suspects that Paul is having an affair and Arianna seems on the verge of leaving.

The finale comes when Paul and Robin separate, and Robin is left to take care of Jonathan without his or Arianna's help. We will have to dramatize fully how Robin finally accepts this responsibility. The pivotal moment can't just be Robin changing Jonathan's diaper and thinking, "Hey, this sure is fun!" Instead, we will want to see Jonathan develop croup in the middle of the night and Robin frantically filling the bathtub with hot water, or perhaps see her

tackle his first birthday party, which involves a roomful of screaming toddlers and red-eyed parents.

After the finale, there will be a dust-settling period in which we
get some sense of how all the events of the novel have affected
everyone in it. This section may be all of a short paragraph, or it
may be an entire chapter. This gives the reader, too, a chance to
absorb the significance of what has occurred, and to formulate a
reaction to it. Your book shouldn't go on too long after the climax,
of course, but exactly how long depends upon the intensity of
that climax. Sure, writers worry (and they should!) about dragging
things out, but the reader will likewise feel cheated if the book
ends too abruptly. We don't need to know everything that is going
to happen to everyone for the next ten years, but we do want
answers to the basic questions. With the basic questions answered,
you can leave some other issues open.

Let's say that in the finale of *Mommies*, Jonathan develops croup
the night *before* his first birthday party. Robin is overwhelmed, but
surprises herself by handling both his nighttime illness and her
daytime guests. When she collapses in exhaustion after folding up
the last piece of wrapping paper, Paul appears on the porch, carrying a bouquet of flowers. Should the novel end there?

Probably not, even though if it does, we may assume that Robin
and Paul will reconcile and live as happily ever after as people do
in this imperfect world. But I'd prefer to see the actual scene of
their getting back together. Both need to assess for themselves,
and therefore for us, what has happened; as they look at their past,
we can anticipate their future. Without that, Paul's return will
seem too convenient, predictable. We want him to be more than a
stick figure, disappearing and reappearing solely to further or to
conclude the story. We want, in other words, for him to be a
rounded character.

I wouldn't have the two of them plan their menus for the next
month, either. By the end of a novel, we should know enough
about them that we can draw some of our own inferences about
the pleasures and problems that lie ahead. The most chilling and
memorable notes of a novel resonate in this ambiguous void, when
readers know enough that they can, with equal conviction, draw
different conclusions about the future.

Narration and Scene

A scene in a novel is not dissimilar from a scene in a play or a movie,
in that it is "seen." The author must describe the events that are

taking place so that we can feel that we are there, not only seeing, but tasting, smelling, hearing and touching.

In *The Art of Fiction*, John Gardner wrote about what he called "the fictional dream." He observed that,

> . . . If the effect of the dream is to be powerful, the dream must probably be vivid and continuous — *vivid* because, if we are not quite clear about what it is we're dreaming, who and where the characters are, what it is they're doing or trying to do and why, our emotions and judgments must be confused, dissipated or blocked; and *continuous* because a repeatedly interrupted flow of action must necessarily have less force than an action directly carried through from its beginning to its conclusion.

Thus the challenge to the author is to create something real that is of course not real. How to do that? By selecting the few details that stand in for the many. The author doesn't describe every breath and heartbeat — that would take forever. The reader needs to be told — specifically — just enough of what's *unusual* that's going on.

This is a skill that takes a long time to acquire, but when the skill is practiced artfully, it is a magical one. An accomplished author can describe how a character flicks a speck of dust from her dress in a way that the reader can imagine volumes more about what that character looks like and what kind of person she is.

A scene simulates real time. We get the impression that events are occurring at that same rate they do in real life, although in fact they will be quickened, because the author will only include what's interesting. Even so, scenes take up a fair amount of space. If your entire novel was written in scenes, it might run a few thousand pages before your characters get through lunchtime.

Fortunately, you don't have to. Alfred Hitchcock is often quoted as saying that, "Movies are like life, with the boring parts cut out." The same applies to novels. Just as your scenes themselves don't include each characters' every breath, neither does your novel include every incident in your characters' lives. Cut out not only the boring things that happen to your characters, but incidents that don't move the story toward its inexorable conclusion (that is, incidents that don't help you prove your premise).

Readers will take certain things for granted. (Shakespeare wisely omitted all of Hamlet's trips to the bathroom.) Often, though, you will need to fill readers in on events that they need to know about but which aren't dramatic or interesting enough to justify an entire scene. These are events you will want to narrate.

Narration compresses action, describing events that occurred habitually, or over a period of time. Narration can go on for many pages, or it can be a sentence. "The year passed quickly," is narration. If nothing particularly worth our attention happened during that year, that sentence may be all we need.

Here is a longer example of narration that might fit into *Mommies* (Robin is speaking):

> Every night that week, Jonathan woke up at one and at four A.M. I was so tired that getting out of bed felt like being exhumed from my own grave—but once I got over that, it was sort of fun. I would watch reruns of "Father Knows Best" while I fed him.

We could go even longer, of course, to convey fully the strain of getting up twice during the night over a period of weeks. Either way, narration is the more efficient technique here, because it simply isn't worth the space to describe a similar incident seven times over.

Conversely, don't avoid scenes when the incident demands them. The discovery of a body, the first time two people make love, the fire that destroys a painter's work—all the pivotal events in the characters' lives deserve to be dramatized for us. How would it be if Tolstoy ended *Anna Karenina* with, "And then poor Anna was so depressed that she did away with herself," and left it at that? What if Hemingway wrote, "They all went to a bullfight and it was exciting"?

In the age of television, novels are more visual than ever, relying more on scenes and less on narration. This isn't an evil phenomenon to be abhorred; in every age, different media affect each other. Besides, a good story will break down into dramatic moments that are easily translated into scenes. Scenes are the bricks of your novel.

But narration is the mortar, and you can use it to move the characters across the globe or twenty years into the future in just a few words.

Point of View

The point of view is the perspective of the writing. At any moment in fiction, the sensory impressions are being filtered through one consciousness, be it the author's or one of the character's. Think of point of view as where the camera is—only it's a camera that can hear, smell, taste and touch as well as see.

In chapter five we defined the first-person point of view: when a character in the novel, speaking as "I," tells the story directly to the reader. Usually the first-person novel is written in a single point of view, which means that one character tells the story throughout, although some novels use more than one first-person narrator, or alternate first- and third-person points of view, to good effect.

In the second-person point of view, a character in the novel addresses himself as "you." The second-person point of view was rarely used until Jay McInerney popularized it in his 1984 novel, *Bright Lights, Big City*, which begins: "You are not the kind of guy who would be at a place like this at this time of the morning." The second person is a variation of the first person, because we are in a single character's head who can tell us only what he knows, and that single character is telling the story, rather than having the story told *about* him, as in the third person.

In the third-person point of view, the action of the story is filtered through a character's head, but that character, instead of addressing the reader directly, is referred to as "he" or "she" or by a proper name. This is a less lively and engaging point of view than the first person, but it also may give us some desired distance from a too-intense or unlikable character. Also, writing in the third person, the author has the additional option of going from the "third-person limited" (in which the camera is imbedded in the character's mind and can only tell us what that character knows) to the "third-person omniscient," in which the camera glides from the character's to the author's perspective.

Writing as an omniscient author, that author is able to furnish us with information that the character may not know. A simple example: "Jane didn't notice the man who followed her home that night." Using an omniscient, multiple point of view, the author has the most opportunities to impart information. But a common trap I see beginning novelists fall into is the tendency to leap from head to head, not only giving us everyone's point of view (including a refrigerator repairperson who appears once), but making those point of view shifts two or three times on a single page. This, I think, is a bigger problem than writing in first person, which I've noted that some editors discourage first-time authors from doing.

There are no better or worse points of view; it depends on you and your novel. The broader the scope of your book—the more complex the story, the longer the time span, the more locations—

the more points of view your are likely to require. But don't go into more characters' heads than needed to tell the story. Going into a character's head may seem like an easy way to establish her motivations, but this is deceptive. Your characters should be able to demonstrate who they are by the way they look, talk and act; too many point-of-view shifts remind us that we are reading and weaken our identification with the character whose head we were last in. (See the chart on page 109 for more on point of view.)

In chapter six we asked, concerning *Mommies Don't Cry*, whose story is this? My answer was that it was Robin's and that I wanted to tell it in the first person. That means that her character will need to have a strong voice, one we can listen to for the duration of a novel. (A good first-person novel, like *Huckleberry Finn* or *Catcher in the Rye*, relies on a strong voice.)

When in doubt, I would encourage the first-time novelist to find one person's story to tell. But that's an individual decision. It all goes back to writing the novel you want to write, which may be the story of several people. Even in a smaller novel, breaking out of a confining point of view might sometimes give your novel the fresh direction it needs (more about this in chapter ten).

If I decide to take Paul or Arianna's point of view, though, not only will they become more central to the story, they will introduce stories of their own. We may find ourselves following Paul to work or Arianna home. That's why, the more points of view, the more ambitious the task you set for yourself: To the extent that *Mommies* gets into the story of Paul's stockbrokerage or Arianna's marriage, those stories will have to affect Robin in some way and will also have to refine and prove the premise. (Introducing those other story lines might change the premise, which is fine, as long as there is a single, clear premise proved when you're finished.)

Many authors don't give enough thought to point of view, which is a powerful tool at the writer's disposal. Imagine *Gone With the Wind* in Melanie Hamilton's head throughout, or *Bright Lights, Big City* in third-person omniscient. Often, as I have said, the point of view you want to use will immediately present itself. Fool around with it if it doesn't.

Voice

For generations writing teachers have been passing on the following wisdom: "Find your voice." These words are so wise, in fact, that they border on the meaningless. After I heard it a few times

Point of View

First Person

Point-of-view character addresses the reader directly as *I*.

- most immediate
- least mobile

Example: "I went to lunch with my editor, and she told me everything that was wrong with my book."

Second Person

Point-of-view character addresses self as *You*. A variation of first person.

- equally immediate
- potentially less engaging, more inner-directed

Example: "You know you should never have lunch with your editor, but here you are."

Third Person

Point of view character referred to as *he*, *she* or by proper name.

- more mobile
- more objective (gives us more distance)

The third person may be used in the following combinations:

Single (may be limited or omniscient) We are in only one character's head throughout the entire novel.

Multiple (may be limited or omniscient) We may be in many different characters' heads at different times during the novel.

Example: "The editor told Donna many things she did not want to hear."

Example: "The editor told Donna many things she did not want to hear. *I hope she's not too discouraged*, thought the editor. *I'm tempted to give up*, Donna thought.

Limited (may be single or multiple) We can only know what the point-of-view character(s) can know.

Omniscient (may be single or multiple) The author gives us information beyond what the character(s) can know.

Example: "Lunch was over in an hour."

Example: "Neither Donna nor her editor could know, that the three-eyed Meegops of the planet Neptune were planning to invade Earth."

I put it in that large hamper marked Easier Said Than Done, along with "communicate constructively" and "floss daily."

The author's voice is easy to recognize, but elusive to describe. It's the spirit of the writing; it's what makes your work as unique as your DNA. With a compelling enough voice, you can get away with anything, from a slow beginning to a thin plot (though your compelling voice is no excuse to try to get away with a slipshod novel).

I have found no better advice for finding your voice than some offered by Muriel Spark in her novel *A Far Cry From Kensington*. A young woman, Nancy Hawkins, who works for a publisher, is often beset by "clever authors of uncertain talent." She suggests to them that they imagine, when beginning their novels:

> "You are writing a letter to a friend," was the sort of thing I used to say. "And this is a dear and close friend, real—or better—invented in your mind like a fixation. Write privately, not publicly; without fear or timidity, right to the end of the letter, as if it was never going to be published, so that your true friend will read it over and over, and then want more enchanting letters from you. . . ."

The more your voice develops, the more personal and unique it will become. Paradoxically, while you are looking for your voice (in the closet? under the bed?) it is also helpful consciously to imitate the style of writers you admire. This isn't plagiarism or copping out—it's actually akin to the way children try on their parent's clothes as they search for their own identities. Your mature voice will echo with your literary heritage, just as our mature identities inevitably bear the marks of our upbringing.

Voice is about taking chances. It's about honesty. It's about calling up someone you hardly know for a date, or making the toast at your daughter's wedding when you think you might be about to cry. It's about going up to the very edge of your despair, figuring the odds at about fifty-fifty that you'll fall in. But it's mostly about patience, which in this case is about turning out a lot of pages that may well end up waiting for the curbside recycling truck.

Setting

All of us are shaped to a large extent by the time and place in which we live. People who lived in Berkeley in the sixties had very different values from people living in London during the Second World War, or children born in the early years of the Depression.

The Germanic tribes that overran the Roman empire had different rules of behavior (not necessarily less strict) than the French aristocracy before the Revolution.

Everything from the food we eat to the pastimes that distract us to the way we raise our children, varies from year to year and place to place. Thus, it is impossible to separate completely your characters and your plot from your setting. If Jude Fawley (from Hardy's *Jude the Obscure*) had lived a century later, he might have applied for a student loan. If Flaubert's *Madame Bovary* had lived in Manhattan in the 1970s, she could have ditched her loser husband and opened a boutique.

If Robin Sovicki grew up on a midwestern farm in the thirties, she never would have gone to college or become a film critic. She might have married young and had babies and prayed that there was enough food for them and herself. But Robin grew up in San Francisco and got married and had a baby in the prosperous but frenetic 1980s. To live up to current standards, she's supposed to be a supermom: have a career, get to aerobics four times a week and serve nouvelle cuisine.

In a good novel, the characters, without sacrificing any individuality, will be woven into the setting. Likewise the plot will be action that couldn't happen in quite the same way anywhere else. Again, Tom Wolfe, in *The Bonfire of the Vanities*, brilliantly captured the interrelationships of politics, law enforcement and the media in 1980s New York to tell a story that could only have happened there. Other cities might have stories to tell of arrogant rich men who lost money and power — *Oedipus Rex* more or less fits that description — but change the setting, and you change the book.

Making use of your setting, a novel can be a powerful instrument for social change. I previously mentioned novels like *The Jungle* and *The Grapes of Wrath*, but other examples include *Uncle Tom's Cabin*, Harriet Beacher Stowe's fictional tract against slavery, and *The Octopus*, Frank Norris's exposé of the Southern Pacific railway monopoly. In these cases, as with *Bonfire*, the setting can become a kind of character itself, driving the action forward.

You don't have to change the socioeconomic structure. The world also needs novels that serve as pure escapist entertainment, and if it is your desire to write one of these books, then go for it, as we so benignly say in my personal setting, California.

But successful popular novels also exploit their settings to achieve their goal of entertaining readers. These types of books often take place in a series of big cities, where the high fashion or film or oil industries are located, where rich and famous people live, and where there are an abundance of restaurants serving radicchio. A good glitzy novel will be as woven into its glamour capital setting as Thomas Hardy's were into the fictionalized English county he called Wessex. (Yes, there is a difference between a good glitzy novel and a bad one.)

Television shows are too often setting-less. After some stock footage of the Space Needle or the Sears Tower, the action moves to a three-walled living room that could be orbiting the globe for all it matters. By contrast, one of the most acclaimed programs in television history, "M*A*S*H," was deeply rooted in its time and place. Even "Dallas" owed some of its appeal to the outlaw legends and mystique of Texas.

If your novel could take place "anywhere, it doesn't matter," you have not yet probed deeply enough into who the characters are. You will create your setting through the details, big and little. Robin and Paul can head out to Muir Woods when they want to get away from it all, then wish they were nearer to it all when they realize they forgot the diapers. The playground will reflect Robin's milieu, in which many mothers work and many children are cared for by nannies. And sure, we might throw in a cable car.

That is not to say that you must be a reporter, scribbling down only the grimy details of real life on planet Earth: A fantasy or science fiction novel may take place in a completely invented locale. But the author of this type of book must describe for us not only what the Klingons or the Hobbits look like, she must also create for us a social, moral and technological context to make the characters interesting and the plot truly gripping. And, like it or not, the author's invention will in some way reflect her own time and place, and the extent to which the author accepts or rejects her own culture.

Whether you are writing about today's headlines or mythical kingdoms, it is your privilege as a novelist to envision the world anew.

TO GET THAT NOVEL STARTED

Learn your craft. Be patient as you master the use of the fiction writer's tools that will enable you to build a novel, one word at a time.

CHAPTER NINE

"But What I Really Want to Do Is Write Novels"

Making the Leap

In *Wild Mind: Living the Writer's Life*, Natalie Goldberg describes her initial confusion when a doctor tells her that he wants to be a writer. She says,

> The way I was brought up, a doctor was *it*! They had money, prestige. They were helping humanity. Then I thought to myself, "You know, I've never met a writer who wanted to be anything else. They might bitch about something they're writing or about their poverty, but they never say they want to quit. They might stop for a few months, but those who have bitten down on the true root do not abandon it, and if they do abandon it they become crazy, drunk or suicidal.

Well, let's not do anything rash.

But I, too, am always amazed at the wide range of professionals who show up at my writing classes: mortgage brokers, lawyers, computer programmers, construction workers, landscape architects — yes, even an obstetrician. And these are in addition to the people I meet in social settings who confide their writing ambitions to me.

Okay, I admit I get a little thrill from being surrounded by this mystique. While I have been trying to demystify novel-writing in these pages — to emphasize that it is a set of skills that must be practiced much like hammering nails or drilling teeth must be practiced — maybe we can keep the ordinariness of writing our little secret.

Now, here's the really fun part: Even other *writers* are in awe of novelists! I most frequently talk to short story and nonfiction writers who tell me that their true ambition is to write novels, but playwrights and screenwriters, too, express the urge. Such is the hold of the novel on people's imaginations, even when our collective attention span has reportedly shrunk to the length of time it takes to read a greeting card.

I guess I couldn't demystify the novel entirely, even if I wanted to. Still, that's what I'm here for, and if novels are what you really want to write, you should write them, whether you are new to writing or you've been practicing another form for years. So this chapter addresses the individual issues that arise for writers from different backgrounds, as well as for a new writer with no background at all.

If You've Been Writing Short Stories

I have heard writers declare that they plan to spend a few years on short stories before they tackle their first novel. Their idea is that, since short stories are shorter, they're also easier. "I figure I should walk before I dance," one student said to me, smiling quaintly.

But this is like studying Spanish when you really want to learn French, on the theory that then it will be easier to learn French, because it will be your second foreign language.

Short stories aren't easier than novels. Yes, they're shorter, no argument there, and you can write and throw away twenty practice short stories in less time than you can write and throw away twenty practice novels. But it doesn't necessarily take more time, or a larger total number of pages, to become a proficient novelist, than it does to become a proficient short story writer.

Let's say you've been writing short stories for a while, either because they seemed less intimidating or because you wanted to practice for writing a novel or just because you like short stories. Now you want to start a novel, maybe even because your writing group keeps complaining that your short stories are so long and rambling.

This is one of those great moments in your life when it pays to not be too good at something, because the more skillfully you can fashion a short story, the more you will have to stretch to break out of the mold.

A short story is about *one person, who, as the result of one incident, undergoes one change.* The moment that person changes is the climax, and everything in the story exists to support that climax. A short story will also have a premise—a point that is proved at the end— just as a novel does.

I observed in the previous chapter that a novel is not a long short story, nor is it a series of short stories that have been strung together. A novel is not only longer, it's wider and deeper: While events in a short story mainly affect the protagonist, those same events in a novel should ripple through all the characters' lives.

Suppose I decide to write a short story about Robin hiring a nanny for her baby. The story opens with her saying good-bye to her husband, who must work the day of the interviews. One by one, the prospective nannies arrive. Robin talks to them but is satisfied with no one. In the end, she decides she must care for her baby herself.

You might not spell out her conclusion for us directly; perhaps you would leave her nursing Jonathan by the window, thinking about some new toy she wants to buy him. Through the careful arrangement of details that create a mood, you can convey a sense of Robin's change, which in this case is a decision. Maybe Robin's husband comes home and they glance at each other in the way of married people, and he nods, tacitly approving her choice.

But you would not give the reader this same sense of closure at the end of a chapter in your novel. You must learn to build momentum from each scene to the next, so that the stakes are continually greater, and our investment in the outcome grows.

To return to our example, Robin is sitting in her chair, humming and nursing Jonathan, and feeling all those gooshy motherly feelings that come with an overabundance of hormones. Paul walks in and she tells him she's decided not to hire a nanny after all, but to quit her job at the magazine and take care of the baby full time. Paul says, "Please don't do that because in three months you're going to be a madwoman, complaining that you gave up your career to change diapers, and I don't think I can take it."

Now Robin might see that he's right, or be angry at his assessment. Either way, this should spur further action on her part.

Maybe Robin and Paul continue to talk, and their talk escalates into a discussion, which is a married-person euphemism for "nasty fight." Then Paul confesses that he hates the firm he works for and is thinking about quitting himself. They can't afford to have both of them unemployed while he looks for a new job.

This is momentum, and it's also what I meant when I said that a novel is wider and deeper than a short story. Robin's decision to work or stay home affects not just her, but her husband and baby. Later, we will see how these decisions affect Arianna as well. *The changes it causes in the other characters will in turn affect Robin again.* For example, Robin gets a raise, and so feels she should give Arianna a raise as well, but then decides not to, and Arianna is angry, which makes Robin feel guilty, which causes her to do something else.

Overall, the novelist's art is a fleshier one than the short story writer's. A short story is likely to be focused very sharply on one aspect of a character's life, but in the course of a novel, we need to see the central characters respond to a variety of situations. Likewise, we need to travel more. A short story often observes Aristotle's unities of time, place and action, while a novel does so rarely. A novel may take place in one day by the sea, but a novelist must be very deft to overcome the boredom that sets in for the reader, watching a few people hang out in the same place for a long period of time.

Get your characters off the phone and into the street. Let them climb mountains so they can see some horizons. Let them go to clearance sales so they can get lost in big crowds. Give us rainstorms, local elections and other natural disasters. Let a few years pass between chapters, just to see what the protagonist looks like with some gray in his hair.

On the level of style, keep in mind that the present tense, which is quite the rage these days, works better in a short story than in a novel. Sympathetic characters are more important in a novel, too. The reason is that both the present tense and unsympathetic characters tend to distance the reader from the material. In a short story that doesn't matter as much, simply because it is shorter, and we are more likely to be reading for the writer's quick, dazzling interpretation of reality. In a novel, we need to get more emotionally involved with what's happening, or we start to wonder, why are we bothering? Never let your reader wonder that.

As a short story writer, when you do sit down to get that novel started, the very length of it may terrify you. Don't think of it as 100,000 words, or 400 pages. Take it one chapter at a time, or one scene at a time, or one word at a time, if necessary.

Finally, from a purely crass, commercial point of view, a well-written novel is actually easier to sell than a well-written short story, at least to major publishers (I'm not counting your school newspaper in this tally), simply because fewer people complete well-written novels. Don't wait if this is the form you want to express yourself in.

If You've Been Writing Nonfiction

The term nonfiction, as I use it here, describes a wide spectrum of writing. At one end are the technical writers of computer manuals or bank brochures, projects that require very different skills from the fiction writer's. Writing a computer manual, for example, the technical writer must not only understand the computer but be able to explain it simply and logically to the person using it for the first time. There are no points to be won for any leaps of the imagination, like comparing the computer itself to "a cat with one, giant eye, stationary and yet moving always."

Other nonfiction writers already use many tools of their fiction-writing siblings. They compress the dialogue of their interview subjects, they use metaphor to convey their meaning more lyrically, and they are adept at selecting details that characterize a person through the senses, like describing the foul odor of the police chief's cigar or the worried look of a movie star in town to promote her memoirs. These are all elements of the "showing, not telling" that is the basis of good fiction.

But nonfiction is still nonfiction, and if that's what you've been writing, you haven't had to invent anything. You've always had the truth both as defense and source: your notes, the home video, eyewitness accounts. The computer works a certain way and no other. The knife had fingerprints on it or it didn't.

Thus nonfiction writers often have trouble breaking away from their habit of documenting the facts. Like most of us, when they sit down to write fiction, they often start with real-life incidents. More than some writers, though, they may then feel confined to what "really" happened, and sometimes cling stubbornly to the notion that everything that *did* happen automatically belongs in the fictionalized version.

And, having written about real people, for better or worse, it is also the former journalist who is apt to feel the most guilt about writing about characters drawn from life.

If you are a nonfiction writer about to make the leap into fiction, keep in mind that fiction is just that. Although you may draw heavily from real life to inspire characters or events, don't forget there are ways to disguise those characters and events. You're not betraying anyone. Writing a novel is not like secretly tape-recording a conversation with your friends and printing it in the *New York Times*.

If the nonfiction you have written has been more of the sales report or appellate brief variety, you will also have to cross the yawning chasm to the language of novels. As a nonfiction writer, you have a solid foundation in grammar and syntax, and that is a valuable one to have; you might be surprised to know how many would-be novelists don't know what a comma is for. Still, you have to practice letting go: living in your right brain, seeing the connection between pillows and flights of birds, eggshells and trees.

A would-be novelist with any kind of writing background has already had to struggle with the discipline of writing. Whether you write blurbs for *TV Guide* or *haiku*, you must ignore the siren song of unwashed dishes and force yourself to face the great abyss that is a blank page. You sit down to do it.

But most nonfiction writers have an additional advantage in that they have had to write with externally imposed deadlines: If the article is due on Monday, then Monday it had better be.

Exploit your own habit of hard work. Too many fiction writers believe they need to contemplate their navels for an afternoon to write the perfect sentence. Better to impose some deadlines on yourself—not for publication, or even necessarily completion, but for turning out numbers of pages, drafts and/or working a set number of hours.

You have also, as a nonfiction writer, developed an ability to choose among available facts and to put them in the most effective order. When the nursing home burns, you know to tell us how a fireman rescued an old man, rather than to write about the clowns-on-velvet pictures that were lost in the lobby.

That's much the same process that a novelist uses when telling the story of his or her characters, except that the novelist gets to *make up* the available facts. Have fun.

If You've Been Writing Stage Plays

Writing a novel after writing a stage play may seem, especially at first, like getting into a hot bubble bath after taking a cold shower.

As a playwright you operate within many restrictions. You can have a stage manager act as narrator or let various characters address the audience directly, but for the most part you must write your play entirely in scenes and tell the story entirely in dialogue.

Set changes and large casts are expensive and cumbersome, so if you write plays for your college drama department or community theater, you probably keep them pretty simple. No scenes of ten thousand slaves building the Great Pyramid for you. Where would you get all those loincloths anyway? Maybe London musicals can have chandeliers crashing, or helicopters landing onstage, but most theaters make do with small budgets. Whatever story you have to tell, you have learned to tell economically, while finding creative and believable excuses to get all those characters to drop over to the house that is your one set.

In terms of plot structure, the length and scope of a play is much closer to that of a novel than a short story, while nonfiction usually has no plot structure at all.

Ironically, then, it's the playwright who may make the easiest transition to writing novels. What you need to do is take advantage of your new freedom. A director may be glad that you've set both acts of the play in the parlor, but a novel will feel stifling in one room. Just like the renegade short story writer, you need to get your characters out under a big sky.

Also keep in mind that the dialogue of a play is subtly different from the dialogue of a novel. You've had to learn to avoid the Soap Opera Trap we discussed in chapter eight; still, the conventions of the theater and the acting ability of the performers allow for more expository exchanges in a play than in real life. Characters in plays are usually a lot more articulate than real people; even uneducated characters must attain a certain simple eloquence because the theater (unlike film) is essentially a verbal medium.

When you write your novel, be sure that your characters don't sound as though they're speechifying. You should narrate (put into straight prose) anything that the characters would not normally say to each other:

> "Do you love me?" she asked.
>
> Christopher did not know how to say that she made him feel like the trailing clouds he saw at sunset, when their bellies glowed with fire.
>
> "Uh, yeah," he grunted. "Sure."

This allows you simply to convey information that is beyond what the characters can express about themselves. Easy? Sure. Something should be.

The theater is also a highly collaborative art form. Once the script is finished, a veritable army of professionals move in to interpret and add dimension to your work, from the director, set designer, lighting designer and stage manager, on down to the actors and actresses themselves. Your stage directions and physical descriptions of the characters have been kept to a minimum so that the director and performers can bring their individual talents to bear. Sure, they can botch their jobs, but still, the play relies—and should rely—on them. When it works the way it's supposed to, this is the great marvel that is theater: a finished production in which the talents of so many professionals come together. In spite of the legendary rivalries among them, theater people are able to produce this magic of cooperation over and over again.

As a novelist, you're pretty much on your own. It becomes your obligation to create word pictures that literally stand in for the work of a dozen or more professionals. There will be no set designer to choose the color of the walls, no director to invent some stage business. You won't be able to rewrite during rehearsals, when you see that something doesn't quite work onstage.

And no matter how laudatory the reviews of your book are, as a former playwright, you are bound to miss the applause.

If You've Been Writing Screenplays

Of all of the writers who tell me they'd like to make the transition to novels, screenwriters surprise me most. The glamour and financial reward associated with films and filmmakers is unrivaled in our present culture.

Like stage plays, movies are the results of the efforts of many professionals, and, like a playwright, the screenwriter builds a kind of scaffold for the director, performers and others to stand on (and then sometimes ends up wishing they'd stand on *another* kind of scaffold).

But of all the forms we've discussed, nowhere does the writer have less control over his or her own work than in the screenplay. This is in part because of the history of movie making; films as an art form owe as much to photography as to scriptwriting. It's also been common since the days of silent films for directors to write scripts as an accompaniment to their directing. The general public can much more easily tell you who directed a film or who starred in it, than they can tell you who wrote it; most screenwriters whose names are familiar to the public are also directors and/or producers. And, although a screenwriter may pitch and eventually sell his or her original script, often they are hired instead to execute the ideas of these same directors and producers.

However, one of the great ironies of screenwriting is that one can make a very comfortable living without ever seeing one's work actually produced. The film industry is a wealthy one, and movies are so expensive to make that the cost of the script is a relatively small part of the overall budget, so it pays a studio to buy many more scripts than it can ultimately use.

By contrast, book publishing is constantly on the edge of bankruptcy and only a small percentage of published novelists can support themselves wholly by writing. Still, once your novel is accepted for publication, the occasional horror story aside, you can pretty much count on its actually *being* published. That, combined with the stamp of "legitimacy," are two strong incentives luring the screenwriter to the novel.

If you are one of those screenwriters so attracted, you have a head start in that you are accustomed to thinking in terms of a strong story and fast pace, two areas in which beginning novelists often go astray. (Would-be screenwriters often believe that snappy dialogue and a visual imagination make for a good screenplay, and it doesn't hurt to have either, but nothing gets calls returned in Hollywood like a well-thought-out story.)

Another fact of life in Hollywood, though, is that the range of films that can be produced is fairly narrow. Once again, making a movie is so expensive that it simply isn't feasible unless the movie, once made, can appeal to literally millions of people. (While the biggest selling book of the *year* may sell less than two million copies in hardcover, and 100,000 is considered wildly successful.) The Hollywood movie, then, tends to deal with fairly basic emotions and proven subject matter. Wars. Sex. Cops and robbers.

As a screenwriter, you've had to think within these limits, and now you will need to fine-tune your sensibilities. That doesn't mean you have to write a turgid, symbolic novel worthy of Franz Kafka, but the typical Hollywood film has a world view that is too simplistic for the novel. Villains and good guys may not always wear black-and-white hats, but they're still hard to miss, from Darth Vader (come to think of it, he *does* wear a black hat) to Tess, the golden-haired secretary in *Working Girl.* The outcomes are pretty predictable, though we may be in suspense about exactly how that outcome will come about: *Rocky* goes the distance, *The Karate Kid* defeats the bullies.

Your novel can certainly have a happy ending—that makes for a more commercial novel—but that happy ending will have to be believable. As movie audiences, we are so conditioned to expect Clint Eastwood to survive, that we don't question it when he walks unscathed from a bus that's had 700,000 bullets fired at it. We're also willing to go along with the idea that a hooker with a heart of gold can become, inside of a week, the sophisticated, cultured, soon-to-be bride of a billionaire industrialist, as in *Pretty Woman.*

When the very same Clint Eastwood/*Pretty Woman* fans pick up a book, they become more skeptical. Since novels are less predictable to begin with, the novelist isn't working with the same set of expectations, and has to make sure that what he or she does deliver to the reader is supported by well-developed characters and a well-documented plot.

Like the playwright, when you make the leap from screenplays to novels, you're on your own. No more cryptic references to "it's an expensively furnished room"—you have to tell us about the rosewood and leather sofa. No glib shorthand about how, "They make eye contact. Sparks." You can get away with a certain level of familiar language in a screenplay; not clichés, but too-lyrical prose would be a distraction. Your novel doesn't have to make Joycean breakthroughs in the use of language, but you no longer have a director, cinematographer and Meryl Streep to complete your vision.

So exploit your ability to draw the reader into what's happening, to dramatize a story in a series of encounters, schemes and confrontations rather than by proselytizing. Then use your own words to make that story, and those people, live.

If You Haven't Been Writing Anything

No previous experience is necessary to learn how to write a novel. And on the positive side, you have no old writing habits to break.

Start by reading as much as you can, especially the types of novels you admire and wish to emulate. You certainly don't need a Ph.D. in literature, but a familiarity with the classics doesn't hurt. It's also good to read books on writing (let's hope so, anyway).

Follow the guidelines laid out in chapters two through seven. Do many of the short writing exercises suggested in chapter three, get used to putting words on paper or disk for gradually longer periods of time. The most immediate hurdle you face will be disciplining yourself to write, but if you are able to do that, you will be as well-positioned as anyone to embark on a writing career.

An introductory fiction writing class, with a good teacher, can be an inspiration. But you don't need to apprentice yourself in poems or short stories or ten years of journal-keeping or staring at the wall. Don't let anyone persuade you to postpone getting that novel started.

TO GET THAT NOVEL STARTED

Use whatever you already know, and build on it.

PART THREE

The Big Mo'

(Pacing Yourself to the End of the Novel)

CHAPTER TEN

The Mid-Novel Blues

The Long Road

Your novel may well be the longest thing you'll ever write. In terms of numbers of words, it is longer than a screenplay and most plays; certainly it's longer than any short story or article. Ph.D. candidates, and some nonfiction authors, also rack up the big page numbers, but there's no question that one of the greatest challenges that faces the novelist is simply staying with a project for the necessary length of time.

Novels are like marriages, marathon runs, Freudian analyses. Novelists therefore cannot afford to be dabblers, dilettantes or commitmentophobes.

Even in the best marriage, there are mornings when you want to put your spouse's face in the Cheerios. The fastest marathon runner isn't always sure he can make it through all those bleak middle miles. And the most dutiful analysand has to deal with resistance and negative transference.

The point is not how to avoid these periods of disillusionment, doubt and boredom, but to recognize that they *are* inevitable, to accept them, to grin about them, and then, not only to survive them, but to use them to learn more about ourselves and our books.

It is this tenacity (a fancy way of saying "hang in there") that distinguishes novelists from many other writers.

That Old Speed Bump Halfway There

I cannot emphasize strongly enough (so I'll have to satisfy myself with repeating) how important it is to know that everyone gets the Mid-Novel Blues. The Blues don't always strike dead in the middle, of course, but that's a common time. There are a couple of reasons for this. The beginning of the book may have come rather easily, only because you've had the basic idea for a while and have been ruminating over the opening scenes. This is the honeymoon. A lot of couples have blissful honeymoons.

Once you get those early chapters down, you have to build on them, something that takes more conscious effort. You've been working hard for what already seems like a long time, and yet here you are with more work ahead than you ever anticipated; you're beginning to realize what you got yourself into.

Put another way, you've done what you knew how to do before you began, and now you have to learn more—not just about your individual novel, but about the skills of fiction writing. It can feel like starting over.

This may also be the time when you've begun showing your work around a little. Maybe you brought your half-filled typing box to a writers' group or conference, and the other writers pointed some things out to you that don't work—things you say to yourself you should have realized on your own. Or they're telling you to chop off the first hundred pages (you're up to page 118), and here you were thinking that the first part was ready to go—you just had to tighten up a scene or two, maybe check to make sure that all the punctuation marks were in the right place.

No matter where you are in your novel, it's easy to get the Blues if you've been submitting other writing (e.g., a short story you completed before you started work on the novel), and it's been coming back to you. Or if someone you know who started writing after you did gets an eight-figure advance from Charles Scribner's Sons.

But the bottom line, the main reason you get the Mid-Novel Blues, is that writing a novel is long and complicated, and you have a complicated relationship with your novel. There are going to be ups and downs. If you write it straight through without any problems, then something is *really* wrong.

How to Recognize the Mid-Novel Blues

Sometimes it's obvious, sometimes not. The most common symptom is that your writing time mysteriously shrinks. Your life becomes hectic, harder. Out-of-town guests arrive. Your other job suddenly becomes more time-consuming. Your boy- or girlfriend gives you an ultimatum about spending weekends with him/her. Your back injury flares up.

Often it's tempting to believe that these external interferences are the real cause of your not writing. It really is tax season, says the accountant. My mother really does need me to come visit, says the daughter.

Other times you will be more honest with yourself. You know that the problem is that you hate the damn thing you call your novel and that you will do anything to postpone working on it. You will phone people you don't like. You will stay late at work. You will go out to buy things you don't need. You will pay bills you don't owe.

You know perfectly well what's going on; you just don't know what to do about it.

If you are a full-time writer, the Mid-Novel Blues may present themselves as any job dissatisfaction does. You don't sleep well at night, and you have trouble getting up in the morning. Your boss seems the most unreasonable person in the world, and because you're your own boss, this puts you in an awkward position.

You think about changing jobs, since it's obvious that you made a mistake in choosing writing as your profession. There are other careers out there, careers that will satisfy your creativity, but provide you with the immediate income and short-term feedback that are so scarce in a novelist's life. Public relations. Architecture. Insurance defense. The typical office seems a paradise: You would have a coffee room stocked with those little packages of instant soup mix, and you would have messages to return, and people to talk to in the bathroom.

Perhaps most insidious of all, the Mid-Novel Blues can come disguised as an idea for a new novel. This idea is so complete and compelling that you know the book would write itself, if you could just abandon the boring, troublesome first novel for it. Artistic rationalization (always a sign of trouble) rears its ugly head: "This is the book I *have* to write," you think, of this second, better, easier idea.

Encounters With the Devil

What do you do? First, *keep your writing time available for writing.* Treat whatever usual hour, or hours, you have set aside to work as sacrosanct, even as you battle the Blues. (You know how difficult it is to carve out that writing time to begin with—you don't want to go through that again.) We'll talk about ways to use that time constructively—but keeping it available is the first step toward acknowledging that the Blues are temporary. Beware of the excuses that would tempt you to do otherwise: "When this trial is over/

when I've moved/when I get a new baby-sitter/when I'm in a good relationship." Sure, there will be some real-life interferences. But if you can find time to get dressed and brush your teeth, you can find time to write *at least* ten minutes a day, which isn't much, but will remind you that you are a novelist at work on a novel.

The full-time writer with a serious case of the Blues can fall deepest into the pit. If you've given up a traditional job to write, you've already invested more, and you correctly feel that you have more at stake. Alone in your writing space, it's easy to doubt many things, including your sanity.

The fact is that writing novels is not for everyone. Ultimately, you will have to decide if you are one of those ones.

Give it time. There is a certainty and a relief that will come with knowing that you gave it your all and that it wasn't for you. (Kurt Vonnegut said, "Talent is extremely common. What is rare is the willingness to live the life of a writer.") Unfortunately, if writing *is* for you, then the self-doubt and anxiety will persist. So when in doubt, hang in there. The Blues pass.

Okay, so what about those of you with an idea for a new novel — the better, easier book you "have" to write?

Don't do that, either. Remember that the Devil can quote Scripture for his purposes. All novels are easy to write until you sit down to write them. It's likely that you will get to the same juncture in the next book and start to have problems similar to the ones that gave you the Blues to begin with. What you've got then are two unfinished novels and plenty of evidence to prove to yourself that you won't get published because you're the kind of writer who can't finish anything.

Not that having an idea for a new novel is bad — quite the opposite. Hold that thought. There will be plenty of time to write number two when you've wrestled number one down to the ground.

Falling in Love Again

So stare down the barrel of your pen into the beloved enemy that is your novel. Use your writing time to try some or all of these exercises. Try them in any order that appeals to you.

Write a Separate Scene About Your Characters

Take your main character, and put him or her in a situation that *you know for sure* doesn't belong in the novel, because it has nothing to do with the story you're telling, or because it involves a new character who you have no intention of including, or even because it strikes you as a dull scene.

Let's say I'm stuck deeply in the mud of *Mommies Don't Cry.* I'm bored with Robin and her problems, and I haven't got a clue about what should happen in the next chapter.

Then I remember that awhile back I had an idea Robin could have an eccentric Aunt Estelle who comes to town to drag Robin to garage sales. I didn't do anything with Aunt Estelle, because I didn't see how she'd fit in. But now is a good time to start writing that scene:

> Aunt Estelle was my mother's older sister, with whom my mother had never gotten along very well. She was a big woman with frosted blonde hair that she wore in the old bouffant style.
>
> Aunt Estelle wasn't poor, but she liked to brag about bargains, and bragging about bargains meant wearing the bargains she bragged about. "See this fur? Genuine fox, and only *eight dollars.*" Never mind that the fur looked like roadkill you'd see on some of northern California's more deserted truck routes.
>
> "Robin," she said to me, as we were waiting for her bags to arrive on Carousel Two, "what you need are some *bargains.*"
>
> Lucky for us, the next day was Sunday. I persuaded El Grumpo (a.k.a. my dear spouse, Paul) to take Jonathan out walking for a while. After that, I figured, he could mindlessly rock the infant seat while the 49ers mugged some other team on TV. Aunt Estelle and I got in the car and cruised the neighborhood with no less dedication than low-riders looking for chicks—except that we were looking for garage sales.

Etc. I'll keep writing about Aunt Estelle as long as she interests me. What's likely to happen is that after a few pages or ten or twenty, I will start to feel a *little* more enthused about going back to brainstorming what actually happens next in That Darned Thing, i.e., my original novel.

It's always possible that the new scene you've started writing *will* end up in your novel, or even lead you to a solution to a plot problem you've been having. But that's not the point. The point is to get reacquainted with your characters in a nonthreatening environment. It's like going out with people from the office for a drink after work. You and your characters have been working long hours on a project that may have started to seem a little tedious, to put it nicely. Cut loose! Shake a leg! The pressure's off. Have your esteemed colleagues in your writing group been telling you that your main character is boring? Who cares? You don't have to address the criticism you've been getting—you just have to write.

Write About Your Characters as Children or Teenagers

For the psychologically-minded among you, this gives you an opportunity to do some digging, though whatever profound insights you come up with about your characters' childhoods is just that much bonus material.

Since Robin's sister Amy is a main character in *Mommies Don't Cry*, I might try writing a scene between them as teenagers that had an effect on them both.

> Amy spent three hours getting ready for her date. I was planning another rip-roaring evening staying home to work on my history paper.
>
> "What do you think, Rob?" Amy didn't have a full-length mirror in her room, but I did, so that gave her an excuse to come in to check herself out, when what she was really doing was showing off her fishnet stockings and miniskirt to me. Why did Mom let her dress like that? I wondered.

This scene is unlikely to be included in the novel, but it might give me a better understanding of Robin's resentment over Amy's teenage popularity. Maybe that in turn will spark new ideas for the current action of the novel.

You don't have to go this far back in time with your characters. Try writing any scene that takes place before the main action of your novel—Amy's wedding, for example, when Robin has the thrill of being her younger sister's maid of honor. Or describe how Robin first discovered she was pregnant.

Change Your Point of View

Take the opening scene of your novel and start writing it from a different point of view. There are a couple of ways to do this. In the case of *Mommies*, I could take the opening scene and switch from first person to third person. To illustrate, I'll use the opening paragraphs we drafted for the novel at the end of chapter six, but do them in the third person.

> Later Robin Sovicki-Decker guessed that she had actually gone into labor about nine in the morning. When she first started getting cramps, though, she remembered the many

warnings she and her husband had received in their Lamaze classes. "You'll be at the hospital a long time," the nurse-instructor had said. "Don't come in any sooner than you have to."

Shortly after noon, Robin was in an office supply store buying typing paper. Suddenly a pain gripped her abdomen. She squeezed the heavy box of paper so tightly that she thought the paper would ooze out. Undignified as it was, she heard herself howl.

"Are you all right?" the cashier asked. He was only about eighteen and trying to grow a beard that so far looked like sandpaper.

Yes, Robin thought, *I always scream like this when I'm feeling fine.* "Can I use your phone?" she asked. The pain had sub-sided so completely that she felt embarrassed, wondering what she had made such a fuss about.

"We don't have a pay phone," the cashier smirked.

Robin looked at the wall phone hanging behind his head. Even though she had been restored to well-being with the passing of the contraction, she decided she'd let the cashier know this was a serious situation.

"Here's twenty cents," she snapped, producing two dimes from her wallet. "But you'd better let me use that phone unless you want to start boiling some water."

Rewriting in a different point of view doesn't just mean chang-ing "I" to "she." You'll discover that you use a different vocabulary and sentence rhythm. Feel free to change any details or events you want. You are rewriting, essentially, and that's what rewrites are for.

If you have been writing from your main character's point of view in third person, you can switch to first. A more radical, but by no means less useful, exercise is to take an entirely different character's point of view, in first or third person. Let's say we want to do the opening scene from Paul, the husband's, point of view. Now we have more choices—we won't just start with the same opening paragraphs, in this case, because Paul wasn't there.

Let's imagine where Paul is. It's noontime, so let's put him at a business lunch. (He could also be in a meeting with a client, or he could be in the men's room, or he could be working out at the office gym—anything we want.) I'll do this in third person, but of course you could do it in first.

Sam Galway, Paul's boss, was on his second martini. Paul, who had lately caught his now-rotund wife's fear of obesity, was waiting for his steamed vegetable plate.

"Decker," Sam bellowed, "we need to expand our client base!"

Sam was drinking more and more at lunch and Paul wondered how he could tell the man who was his boss that he had a drinking problem.

When the maître d' approached, Paul fleetingly expected him to ask him and Sam to leave, even though the tipsy Sam had made no public display. Instead, the maître d', looking funereal, leaned over and whispered to Paul, "Important call for you."

Any other time, Paul would have assumed it was Mrs. Sherman, a small investor who liked to track him down in strange places so she could ask him to quote the most recent price of all the stocks she owned. This week, though, there was only one thing an important call could be.

He was right. "Your wife just phoned," his secretary told him. "She said you should meet her at Children's Hospital."

These are particularly good exercises to do if you have had doubts about the point of view you've chosen. Maybe you've gotten too close to a character, staying just in his or her point of view, or maybe you've tried to do too much, following half a dozen characters through the maze of a book.

I'm not suggesting that permanently switching or adding points of view is the solution to the Mid-Novel Blues, though sometimes it will be, and discovering that might be the bonus of this exercise. What I am suggesting is another way to take a fresh look at your characters and what's happening to them.

Write That "Other" Novel (for a While)

One of the more common symptoms of the Mid-Novel Blues is a choking sensation and a rigidity in your arms at the thought of writing whatever the next scene in your novel should be. With the above exercises, you aren't writing the next scene. You're writing a scene that won't add to the word count.

But sometimes you just need to get away, even from people you love. If the above exercises seem as overwhelming, impossible and stressful as working on the novel itself has been lately, go ahead and start working on your next novel.

No, I am not contradicting myself. I realize that I just warned you against abandoning your current novel for a younger, prettier second novel. The warning stands as written; you and your first novel need to work things out.

If you do have an idea for a second novel, though, here's how to use that to your advantage. Have yourself a fling: Take a break from your first novel and use your writing time to jot down notes or character bios or even an opening scene for your next book. That's a different story from junking novel #1 to pursue novel #2 with the illusion that it will be easier than the first.

This keeps you writing, and after a while you'll feel more relaxed, and ready to fight the good fight with #1 again. Meanwhile, you've collected some material to file away that you can take out when you *have* finished #1 and are ready start #2 in earnest.

If you approach it with this attitude, collecting this material reaffirms, rather than undermines, your self-image as a writer. That little pile of pages tells you that you will survive this novel, and go on to write yet another one. Why it's already waiting! Meanwhile, once again, you have turned down the heat. You haven't actually started to write #2, so what you put down on paper doesn't have to be divinely inspired.

Review the Exercises in Chapter Three

Writing is a process in which we revisit our beginnings over and over again.

Maybe you don't have an idea for a second novel yet, or maybe you're just sick of anything with the label "novel" attached to it. Then use your writing time to go back and do some of the "what to write about when you've got nothing to write about" exercises outlined in chapter three. Hopefully, along the way, you've added to that list with some ideas of your own.

If you need them, though, here are two brand-new suggestions:

1. Pretend you're an animal, and write about your life. Write about what grass tastes like, how it feels to have people ride on your back, or the sensation of bark under your paws when you climb trees.

2. Write about a journey. Say where you're going and what you've packed. Describe the people on the bus or airplane or in the car.

Write about whatever you want, looking outside yourself for sensations and details. Paint an outer landscape that corresponds with the inner one, but don't just write about how depressed you are about your writing.

Take a Break

Desperate times require desperate measures. Yes, in spite of all I've said, there may be a time when you need to take a few days off from your work. During that break, you can use your regular writing time to do some novel-related things you've wanted to do, like trekking to the library to look up some fact you need or filing papers or cleaning up your office or interviewing someone.

If you really can't even face that, *use the writing time to play.* Have lunch with the gals or a beer with the guys, hit the bowling alley or a matinee. But don't let the rest of your life take over! Don't start using the writing time to mow the lawn or to grocery shop.

Try going somewhere by yourself. Some writers swear by long, solitary walks in bucolic surroundings as a way of generating new creative thoughts. They like to sit on big boulders overlooking the ocean or drive out to the woods or hike up a mountain. You can do any of the above for fun, or you can do it for the good of your novel.

If you start to feel guilty about not writing, then act on that. Guilt is a good motivator. In my family, it's like rocket fuel.

Lest you think I sound like a completely fanatical madwoman (I hope I do, actually), let me say that after you've been writing seriously for a year, you can relax your obsessive hold on yourself somewhat. It will always be important to be disciplined, but gradually that discipline will become a part of your personality. The weight of the writing behind you will always be there to give you a little momentum, so that if you have to move, or decide to travel for a month, it will be easier to return to a productive schedule. (But don't move or travel if you can help it.)

During the first year of writing, be a fanatic. You've spent a lifetime of *not* writing, and it's easy to slide back into that. So after a few days off, pick up with your ten minutes a day, or more.

Human Contact

The Mid-Novel Blues aren't so different from any other kind of blues. This is when we need help from our loved ones. Seek it out; you know who supports you, who'll help you keep going.

Other writers with more experience are the best people to reassure you that you can ride out the Blues. They may also be able to suggest concrete solutions to specific problems that are bogging you down in the novel. "Get more of the characters together in the party scene—that'll speed things up." "Let Jeff have more confidence, and we'll care about him more." Hopefully, you already know or can find a sympathetic and intelligent reader.

This is not a good time, though, to send the first part to your friend's agent who promised to read it, nor is it a good time to walk into that new writing group of sharp-tongued MFAs with a reputation for eating beginning novelists for breakfast. A callous response to your efforts is harder than usual to take when you've got the Blues, and will only prolong them.

What the Blues Can Teach Us

Anyone can write when the ideas are flowing, and the characters are behaving. It's just like when you first fall in love: Everything your beloved does is adorable — even the long noisy slurps he takes of hot coffee — and everything he says is wise, even that old story about the priest, the minister and the rabbi. When you live with someone for a period of years, not only do the slurps get louder, but it seems you've heard the same jokes 1,817,299 times.

But it is also over a period of years that you can develop a truly reliable commitment with another person. You have a history. She knows you better than anyone, so you might just as well be yourself. It isn't because things are always easy, but each crisis you and your partner survive can make the bond between you stronger, if each of you is willing to try harder and to compromise.

So each time you get the Blues (yes, it can happen more than once in the writing of a novel) keep writing anyway. Each time you struggle until you master the higher level of skills you need to meet the growing demands of your book, you become more proficient and stronger as a writer. You learn that you are capable of meeting ever-greater challenges. When the Blues come back, you can greet them as a respected adversary, if not a friend.

Hang in there. That's a colloquial way of saying, "be tenacious."

TO GET THAT NOVEL STARTED
(and keep that novel going)

Keep writing *even when your novel bogs down. Recognize that lean creative times are part of the package.*

CHAPTER ELEVEN

The Joys of Second (and Third, and Fourth) Drafts

More Good News/Bad News

The bad news is that you are not going to churn out a seamless, polished, get-rich-and-famous novel in one draft. The good news is that no one does, and you don't have to, either.

When I was his student, Leonard Bishop used to say to us, "The only reason your novels aren't publishable yet is that they aren't finished yet."

You, the writer, need to know at the beginning that there will be an end. The focus of this book is getting started, but there's no point in getting started if you're not going to finish.

So in this chapter I will give you some guidelines for getting through that first draft, and then identify some of the common problems you will want to correct in your second.

One Draft Straight Through

You've got to get some clay before you sculpt a statue. You've got to whip up some batter before you bake a cake. Therefore, my usual advice to beginning novelists is to write a first draft straight through.

A common pattern is for an author to write the first two chapters, then take them to a writing group or to show them to an instructor for feedback, and then to rewrite them. That's fine. The author frequently must experiment to find a correct tone or direction for the novel. Also, it isn't bad to see how well you are able to incorporate the suggestions that others make.

But after one or two rewrites, *max*, of those opening chapters, you need to move on and write chapters three through whatever. The first two chapters may be far from ready, but in fact, the only way you can *get* them ready is to write the middle and the end of the entire book. In the writing of an entire draft, you will first of all make many discoveries that lead to changes in your original conception of the novel. Maybe I'll realize that Robin's career as a film reviewer doesn't put as much pressure on her as I want, and I'll decide to make her a chiropractor. What a drag if I've already rewritten the first chapter so many times that I can't stand to look at it anymore.

I'm also likely to get to know Robin as a character better through the process of living with her in a variety of situations. There's a limit to how deep I can go with her in just those opening chapters. You might get to know your piano teacher very well as a piano teacher, but to know her in some other capacity, you have to get her away from the piano and into a nightclub or the kitchen or to a racetrack.

Writing a first draft straight through isn't a shortcut, any more than anything else I've suggested. Would to God there *were* some! No, you will have plenty of time to write and write and rewrite. Writing straight through is one way, though, to make sure you are moving forward. Although it's certainly better to rewrite the beginning than to stop writing, if you are constantly reshuffling and reconceiving the opening chapters, you are avoiding the unknown, unwritten chapters—a very subtle form of writer's block, or the Mid-Novel Blues in disguise.

In Leonard's workshop we used to have a party for anyone who finished his or her first draft. It was a way of acknowledging someone for passing an important milestone. There was still work to do, but the author had, in a sense, become just that—an author.

Okay—you won't always be able to write straight through. When the Blues strike, you'll do whatever you have to do to beat them back. In addition to the suggestions outlined in chapter ten, sometimes it helps to skip ahead and write a scene you've been looking forward to writing, or even to write the end if you think you know what that is. If you don't know the end, or there is no scene you've been looking forward to writing, write any scene that you think comes later in the book. Set that scene aside for when you need it, and plug it into the draft when you catch up to it later. The edges may not fit exactly, because your novel will still be in a state of flux. Plug it in as best you can.

The Baddest Draft in the Whole Darn Town

One of the best ways to get started is to give yourself permission to be bad. So be b-a-a-a-d. Write the baddest darn draft you can come up with, if that's what keeps you going. Don't edit. You actually don't *know* what's bad or good yet.

As you go through that first draft, you will often have to ask yourself for permission to be bad all over again. That's because there will be days when you can't believe just how poorly you are writing, just as there will be days when the words dangle in the air for you to grab, when they snap together for you in dazzling new combinations.

Again, as you get feedback, don't worry too much about rewrites, but do try to apply what you hear to future chapters.

When you've finished the first draft, go back and read the whole thing. By now the beginning especially will seem as though someone else wrote it, and you can read it more objectively. Here are some of the things you should look for:

First of all, search out and destroy anything that even remotely resembles a cliché. The only really true absolute in fiction writing is that you never use clichés.

A cliché sticks out like a sore thumb. It's like a red flag, and your reader is the bull. Your book can't fly like an eagle, if you use expressions that are as old as Methuselah.

Pretty awful, huh? Clichés are to prose what stereotypes are to character: death. (Who *was* Methuselah? How old *was* he?)

Other clichés: Her heart sank. His face fell. She couldn't see the forest for the trees. The name rang a bell.

The cliché that makes me shudder as if I've bitten into a rotten strawberry (notice I didn't say "the cliché that really gets my goat") is "sparkling eyes." I once heard a writer defend her use of that expression. "But Grandpa really did have sparkling eyes," she insisted, and then added, "I suppose I should have made that clear."

Ah, yes, the sad thing is that clichés began as original, fresh phrases. What a lovely image — sparkling eyes! One might imagine how the pupil somehow multiplies the light it reflects. But the image has now been used to the point where it no longer conveys any meaning. Trust me — readers will not meditate on the image of sparkling eyes, nor will they stop to tease out the nuances of the image of a young girl with "a spring in her step." Confronted with such familiar expressions, readers skip ahead to the next sentence while registering nothing but a vague sense of boredom.

Even the cliché rule has a narrow exception: A character can use the occasional cliché in dialogue, because in real life, real people use clichés. But even then, use them very, very sparingly, because clichés are extremely tedious to read. A character who relies on them too heavily will not be an interesting character. Sure, you may have a character who's not supposed to be interesting; just remember that we won't need to spend very much time with that character to be convinced of how uninteresting he or she is. Why should we read about uninteresting characters at all, when we can watch "The Brady Bunch" in syndication?

It takes awhile before your Cliché Detector can pick up the low frequencies. There are less obvious—but hardly less trouble-some—glib, familiar expressions that lie flat on the page: *She searched high and low. There wasn't a soul in the room. A little goes a long way.* People will point these phrases out to you, and looking for them in other's work will make you more sensitive to them in your own.

Declare your novel a Cliché Free Zone. When you come across a cliché or familiar expression, take it out. If necessary, replace it with something more original and specific. If you see that you've written "her heart sank," then ask yourself, what can this character do to convey the disappointment I want to convey? Or maybe her disappointment is so apparent that you don't need to tell us about it at all.

Vague adjectives contain smaller doses of the same poison as the cliché. Vague adjectives include: *good, bad, ugly, pretty, nice, beautiful, wonderful, terrible, handsome, great, lovely.* These are value judgment words, which convey the author's opinion without any concrete information to allow the reader to decide for himself whether or not to agree with that opinion.

When you see a word like "wonderful," take it out and replace it, if you need to, with *what* was wonderful. Say you've written, "the party was wonderful." Why? Because you met a tall, blonde woman who said she'd love to have dinner with you? Because the hostess served your very favorite pineapple-and-bacon hors d'oeuvres? If you've already included those details, you don't need to tell us, on top of that, that the party was wonderful. We know.

Somehow, clichés and vague adjectives find their way into first drafts. They're like those extra wire hangers in your closet: No-body's really sure how they get there. Your job, though, is to get rid of them.

Another "wire hanger" to look for in your first draft is the recap sentence. These are a symptom of a tendency to draw a conclusion unnecessarily for the reader, and their natural habitat is the last line of a paragraph. As in:

Norman had been preparing for the trial all week, working fifteen-hour days, and eating, when he even took time to eat, bags of peanuts at his desk. When he came home Friday night, his shirt was wrinkled and his hair needed combing. There were dark circles under his eyes, and he could hardly lift his briefcase as he climbed the stairs. He was tired.

If you guessed (correctly) that you can cut the final sentence — "He was tired." — give yourself a hand.

Our earlier example of the use of a vague adjective, "The party was wonderful," could also be a recap sentence, if you made it the last sentence of a paragraph, after describing the stimulating company and haute cuisine at a social gathering. Either way, you can nuke it.

Unlike the wire hangers in your closet, though, the clichés, vague adjectives and recap sentences that show up in your writing will diminish over months and years, if you show them no mercy now.

Scenes We Don't Want to See — or It's Deja Vu All Over Again

In your second draft you will also want to look for redundant scenes, that is, scenes that accomplish the same thing storywise as an earlier scene. For example, let's say I have a scene early on in *Mommies* in which Robin breaks down and cries when Jonathan gets her up at 4 A.M. and won't go back to sleep. Fine — I've shown her responding to a certain kind of pressure in a certain way. Now, it would be a waste of space (and a waste of the reader's time) to write essentially the same scene two chapters later, showing how Robin breaks down and cries at the sight of diaper rash. Those are new "facts" — a different problem, a different day — but no new "information": Jonathan is the same baby, doing the same baby things, and Robin is the same person, responding the same way. Having shown Robin crying when she is tired and feels incompetent, she should be either markedly worse or markedly better the next time she is tired and feels incompetent. So she'll either handle the diaper rash or it will send her to a hospital.

Miscellany

Look for long explanations that will bog the reader down. How can you break them up, or dramatize the same information? For example, rather than read a long passage of narration about how Robin and Paul aren't getting along these days, give us one good scene of them fighting about something specific.

Look for anything that's so obvious that you don't need to explain it ("Since this was her first baby, Robin was excited and scared"). Conversely, look for areas that are fuzzy, unclear or contradictory. Remember that the reader doesn't know anything about you or what you want to say—the reader can only know what you've put on the page. Of course you don't want to be simplistic or obvious—but if your main character is a liar and a thief, readers will not also guess that she is a good person underneath it all, unless you give them some evidence (such as, the character uses the money he steals to help the poor).

Look for mixed metaphors. "There was an emptiness inside her that burned," is a mixed metaphor, because "emptiness" can be hollow or deep, or maybe black and cold, but it doesn't burn.

Look for passive voice, which arises in a construction that uses the verb to be, and shows the speaker acted upon rather that acting. If you write, "Amanda was frightened of Clark," that will be less gripping than "Clark frightened Amanda."

One of the main things you have to look for, and usually take out, is the flashback. This is such a pervasive problem in first novels that the subject deserves its own section so I can rant and rave about it properly.

Flashbacks: the Pause That Depresses

I've several times warned about the dangers of getting too attached to background material and therefore including that background material unnecessarily in the novel. Far too often first-time novelists include huge sections of flashbacks, especially in the beginning of the book. The author believes, firmly and passionately, that the reader needs to know how the characters got to be the way they are, and that the only way to do that is with flashbacks.

An illustration from *Mommies Don't Cry* would be if, after showing Robin giving birth, instead of coming home with the baby and getting on with the story, I decided to flashback to Robin's growing up, describing her parents' marriage, showing how she and Paul met, whatever.

I can always find a way to justify flashbacks. I can reason that the best way to get to know Robin is by telling us what her life has been like up to this point. I can argue—forcefully, if need be—that we need to see her parents' marriage as a contrast to her own.

I'd be wrong.

The hard, unavoidable truth is that the reader wants to know what's going to happen *next*. Meanwhile, I'm going for something easy: I know Robin's background, I can summarize it, I can even write scenes about it, but I don't have to worry about linking it up with the main action.

That is not to say that an author cannot go back and forth in time. This is an ambitious structure that, when skillfully done, can result in a more powerfully told story, one that stretches our understanding of cause and effect.

What you need to do, though, is to distinguish between telling a story that is not chronological, and padding a book with flashbacks. Here's how: If a flashback exists solely to characterize, you don't need it. I don't care how interesting the material is, or how well-written it is, you don't need it.

You don't need it.

One way to determine whether your flashback exists solely to characterize is to ask yourself if you could significantly alter the content of the flashback without changing anything outside the flashback. Example: I write a flashback describing Robin's feelings as she watches Amy get married, hoping to shed light on their current relationship. But I could just as easily write a scene of the two sisters playing a desperate game of Scrabble, or show them at camp having their first crushes on boys in the cabin across the lake, without changing anything I've planned to write, according to our outline, in the rest of the book. Since it doesn't affect the story, it exists solely to characterize.

If, in spite of my wise words, you are thinking, "She can't possibly mean *my* flashback—it's so funny and revealing and I worked so hard on it, that I must keep it!" then consider this: Flashbacks in the first part of novels are so overused, that they are like sandwich boards passing under the noses of editors, announcing, *This is an amateur job*. When an editor gets to them she sighs, and mentally, if not literally, puts the manuscript away. So get rid of the flashback and get on with the present story.

When You Can Get Away With It

To illustrate how a flashback does affect the story, let's go back to one of the examples I just cited, in which I show Robin and Amy at camp. If it turns out that the boys they had crushes on return to terrorize them twenty years later, and Robin rescues Amy, or vice versa, and this causes the sisters to realize how much they need each other, you might have a relevant flashback.

Here are two more examples of flashbacks that further the story as well as characterizing the people in it: Let's suppose we read the bulk of *Mommies* believing that Robin is a good, misunderstood wife and Paul a too-withdrawn spouse. Then, three-quarters of the way through, we learn through a flashback that Paul is not actually Jonathan's father, though he doesn't know it. That piece of information will dramatically change our perception of the events and characters thus far, and could certainly justify a scene written as a flashback. To truly function, though, *the revelation should lead to further story complications*. Paul will find out; Robin will try to make amends; their relationship will flounder or grow stronger.

Another example would be if Robin learned halfway through that she herself had been adopted. That would not only deepen our understanding of her insecurity as a mother and her discomfort with her own mother, it could cause her to take more action — for example, she might search for her biological parents. Again, a flashback must have a concrete effect.

Even in the above two examples, we could get the necessary information in various other ways. Robin could confess the secret of Jonathan's paternity to his pediatrician, because it would be relevant to the baby's health; or Frances, Robin's mother, might admit that Robin was adopted after Robin pesters her with endless questions about her own infancy. Dramatizing an event in the present is almost always preferable to a flashback, in part because a flashback disrupts the "vivid, continuous" reality of your novel.

I've mentioned that authors mostly succumb to the temptation of flashbacks in the first part of their novels, but that doesn't mean that saving the same flashback for later in the book makes the flashback work better. Sorry — if it doesn't belong, it doesn't belong. As it turns out, though, writers themselves are more selective about the flashbacks they include later in their books, because by that time they're usually so engrossed in the story that they don't want to slow it down with unnecessary trips to the past.

If you've already written reams of flashbacks (presumably before you started reading this book), don't worry about it now. Keep writing your first draft. When you've completed that first draft, go back and be brutal with your delete key or red pencil. It will be easier to cut thirty pages from the novel when you've written 300, and it also may be clearer to you by then that the novel *doesn't* need them.

The Parallel Story Structure

I do want to illustrate a way in which going back and forth in time can work, so let's re-envision the plot of *Mommies* for a moment.

Suppose I have two stories going simultaneously—one in the "present" (still written in past tense) and one in the past. The present story is the same as we've already outlined, except that the chapters that take place in the present now alternate with chapters describing Robin's growing up, competing with her brother and sister for their parents' attention, trying to find a subject in school that she can excel in, etc.

This can work if: 1.) the story set in the past fulfills all the requirements for a well-plotted story: conflicts leading to other conflicts until a premise is proved; 2.) the present and past stories link up at some point; and 3.) the two stories together prove a single premise. Example: the premise of Robin's story as we've discussed it is that motherhood makes you a stronger person. Let's refine that a little. What is it particularly about motherhood? Maybe in the context of this novel, it is being forced to be unselfish that makes you a stronger person.

The story of Robin's growing up might then be the story of her constantly fighting for her own interests, which constantly leads to disappointment. That proves the other side of the same premise: Selfishness makes you a weaker person.

This two-story structure will be even stronger if the same story question is central to both. Maybe Robin's learning she was adopted in the present story, toward the end of the novel, is what finally enables her to make sense of the story of her growing up, as well as to become a better mother in the present.

Another example of a two-story novel would be a murder mystery that simultaneously traces the detective's investigation in the present and goes back in time to tell the story of the early life of the victim. The question, "Who did it?" is central to both tales, which will link up when we learn the answer.

Novels that use this structure successfully include *Paradise Postponed*, by John Mortimer, and *The Prince of Tides*, by Pat Conroy. Allow me to observe that neither are first novels. But if writing a novel in this form sings to you, then that's what you should do.

Surviving the Second (and Successive) Drafts

Like a root canal, the Bar Exam and car trips with toddlers, second drafts can seem pretty overwhelming. Unlike those other adventures, they usually don't turn out to be as bad as you fear. In fact, once you get started, you will probably find your second draft much easier than your first.

As you re-read that first draft, make notes about what you want to do in your second. Then go do more homework exercises (see chapter six) if necessary. You will have identified the weak areas that need more thought. If you've already done the bios, focus on monologues and/or interviews. Feel free to do more monologues and/or interviews, exploring new territory, or to fine-tune your bios.

Now is the time to articulate your premise, if you haven't already, and now is the time to hammer out a more detailed, workable outline. It's good and proper to feel your way through a first draft, but by the second draft, you want to map out some strategy.

Using even a very rough first draft as raw material, you should be able to come up with an outline that's far more specific than what you've had up to now (that outline will be for you, by the way—scene-by-scene outlines aren't of much interest to editors). There may still be some problems you're simply not able to solve yet, but it's time to make some decisions, too, about what the work is going to be about.

Then, start your second draft the way you started your novel: *start*. You will be amazed at the skills you have acquired. Writing will still be a struggle—boring at times, aggravating at others—but just as a first draft has its particular rewards—the moments of ecstatic discovery when the characters give *you* ideas—so does the second draft provide you with times when you know you are becoming a craftsperson. Some of the changes you need to make will take care of themselves. You'll be writing and you'll say, "Ah ha— *that's* how I can make Cathy more sympathetic."

Get That Novel Finished

Certainly the most efficient way to write a novel is to write first one draft, then another, then another, then—well, I don't want to scare you, but you get my point. Too often beginning writers do a couple of hasty drafts and start calling agents. They end up with boomerang books that land on their desks again and again.

I asked James N. Frey how many drafts he does. "Four or five," he told me, "but I go through the manuscript and make small changes dozens of times for each draft."

The author Brad Newsham (*All the Right Places*) said, "I did four complete drafts of my first book. Saying four drafts might be misleading, however. I did almost constant tinkering."

And another novelist, Barbara Brooker (*So Long, Princess*): "I'm a perpetual draft writer. It's like layering sweaters on a cold day."

Here is some of John Gardner's advice for perfecting a novel:

Read [it] over and over, at least a hundred times—literally—watching for subtle meanings, connections, accidental repetitions, psychological significance. Leave nothing—no slightest detail—unexamined; and when you discover implications in some image or event, oonch those towards the surface.

Novels take a long time. But unless you only want to write one, or you believe in reincarnation, don't turn your first novel into your entire life's work, either. *Beware of rearranging furniture in a third or fourth draft.* At a certain point you have to commit yourself to a certain sequence of events and work with them. Remember that you will write more than one novel.

Set a daily page quota—whether it's one, five or twenty pages will depend on how much time you have to write and how much rewriting you have to do. You won't always fill your quota, and don't beat up on yourself when you don't. You certainly don't want to make your quota at the expense of revamping something in the novel that needs revamping—no one will ever reward you for a too-superficial rewrite. But the quota gives you something to shoot for. If you're writing a novel that's approximately 400 pages long, by writing five pages a day, you can do an entire second draft in 80 days, or 9½ weeks. Now, that doesn't seem so terrible, does it?

Be prepared: Levin's Rule of Rewriting is that you have to do one more draft than you think you can stand. But each successive draft will be much less of an overhaul than the one before. Don't worry. There will be an end.

TO GET THAT NOVEL STARTED
(and be sure to get it finished)

Don't forget that you'll have plenty of time to make it "good enough," and that's just what you'll do.

CHAPTER TWELVE

You're Not on Your Own, Kid

The Loneliest Profession

Just as the three most important elements of real estate are *location, location, location,* the three most important rules of writing are — yep — *keep writing, keep writing, keep writing.* You can read books, you can take classes, you can sit in cafes and smoke thin brown cigarettes and argue about whether the Minimalists will endure — but nothing substitutes for the agony, the loneliness, or the transcendent joy of the act of putting words on a page.

Nevertheless.

There's something else you need to do, and although it isn't as important as the writing itself, it's a close second. That something else is joining a community of writers.

We've talked about the frustration of not getting an immediate response to your day's work. A writer friend of mine bought one of those speakers that plays canned laughter at the push of a button, but said it just wasn't the same. As for me, at times I've longed for a boss to bark orders over my shoulders.

Most people who are drawn to writing novels in the first place have the souls of novelists. They are naturally reflective and inner-directed. Still, the isolation of writing remains one of its built-in challenges. That much aloneness is going to stress the nerves of the world's biggest hermit.

Yet the essential — dare I say *existential?* — loneliness of writing a novel cannot be changed, nor should it be, because it goes to the heart of what a novel is: the unique expression of one consciousness. A screenplay or a stage play may be written with others, in part because the finished product will be the result of a multiperson effort; so, too, journalism may be the product of more than one mind. But you can't have it both ways: You can't have singularity of vision and company at the same time.

What we can and must do is to balance some of this isolation by seeking out colleagues. If you are a nurse, a legal secretary or a teacher, you go to a hospital, office or school every day to work. At some point you congregate at the nurse's station/coffeemaker/ teacher's lounge to grouse about the patients/clients/students and/ or the doctors/lawyers/principal.

But if you are a novelist, you may be putting on your bathrobe and shuffling over to the PC. At breaktime, you talk to your cat. And if you have another job, and your co-workers know you are writing a novel, their idea of emotional support might be to razz, "You've been working on that book two months already! When are we going to see you on 'The Tonight Show'? "

You need to know that you are not the only one who has set out on this crazy, indefensible, miraculous path.

Where the Crazy People Go

You can start with an introductory class at your local community college or university extension program. Ask among your friends if they've taken any writing classes, or know anyone who has.

In classes like these, you will meet other beginning writers, and you will also have an opportunity to talk to the instructor about further resources, and ongoing groups, available in your area. The ongoing groups—about which more later—don't always advertise, so you may have to learn about them through word of mouth.

Another good way to meet fellow writers is the writers' conference. Most writers' conferences are held during the spring and summer; they may be two days to two weeks long. Anywhere from 20 to 500 writers gather in the mountains or by the sea to exchange manuscripts and to listen to authors, editors and agents talk about everything from the most elegant use of dependent clauses to how many extra copies you can sell if your book has a picture of a naked woman on the cover.

A writers' conference is an intensive experience, not always for the squeamish. You might want to start out with a class or a one-day seminar first; that is, a shorter-term commitment that allows you to go home and clutch your teddy bear afterwards.

When you're ready, though, sharing the intensity of a writer's conference is a good way to make friends who are also fellow soldiers. You'll all need each other in the years to come.

Writers' conferences are often sponsored by colleges or universities, or they may be independently run by profit or nonprofit agencies. Get a copy of the May issue of *Writer's Digest* magazine, or the annual *Novel & Short Story Writer's Market*, for a list of yearly conferences, then write for brochures. (Many writers' conferences also advertise in *Poets & Writer's* magazine throughout the spring.)

Then choose carefully. Writers' conferences run the gamut from the complete rip-off to the once-in-a-lifetime experience. Here are things to look for:

1. *A knowledgeable staff.* This doesn't necessarily mean famous. Teaching fiction and writing fiction do not require the same skills or talents; a university position should impress you as much as a best-seller.

2. *Longevity.* If the conference has been held for a number of years, that's a good sign: It means that it has a decent reputation and keeps attracting students. (It's only a sign, though: New conferences won't necessarily be bad, and some of the best conferences sink only for lack of funds.)

3. *Testimonials.* Whenever possible, talk to one or more people who have been to this particular conference in the past, and see if they were pleased with the experience. You can start by asking the instructor and anyone else in your writing class if they've been to any conference they can recommend.

4. *Location.* Writers' conferences are held all over the country. Choose one that is likely to have attendees from your area, who will be easier to keep in touch with later.

5. *Feedback.* Determine what the format is for getting your work critiqued. Some big conferences are mostly a series of parties, speeches and panel discussions; others divide participants into smaller groups to discuss individual manuscripts under the leadership of one of the staff members.

6. *Contacts.* See if you can find out what opportunities you will have to talk to the staff, in addition to your formal critique. Obviously, one of the things your are looking for at a writers' conference is an opportunity to collect the names of Real Live Agents and Actual Breathing Editors with whom you can discuss your novel and to whom you can later send the completed manuscript.

The point of a writers' conference is hardly to polish apples, of course. The point is to meet other writers and publishing professionals, and to hear what they have to say about their experiences. Hopefully, you will find kindred spirits among them. With luck, at a writers' conference, in a matter of days, you can find comrades-for-life, make contacts, get feedback and take a vacation.

Yet Another Myth

Writers' conferences have their limitations, as well: There's only so much you can learn, about craft in general or your book in particular, in two weeks or less. For that reason, you also need to find a way that works for you to get more regular feedback.

They say that writing can't be taught. Well, it can't. But it *can* be learned.

I make that distinction because it's true that no one can tell you how to write your novel, or how your style should develop. And, while a dedicated composition teacher might briefly excite a class of high school students over the beauty of a well-turned phrase, no teacher in the universe can make a novelist out of someone who doesn't desperately want to be one.

You can, however, by your openness and willingness, and desire to master your craft, avail yourself of trained responses to your work to see strengths and weaknesses that you would otherwise miss. In fact, it's crucial that you do. Otherwise, you can write draft after draft, and your writing will not grow, even though you are reading good novels and good how-to-write-novel books.

Few people are completely self-taught in any field. In fact, there are a number of excellent graduate programs that offer either MFAs in creative writing or MAs in English with an emphasis in creative writing. These programs have become increasingly popular with would-be authors since the 1960s, and for good reason. While you study, you can live like a student (i.e., cheaply), and a certain amount of writing time is built into your schedule. It's a natural setting in which to find a mentor, and you end up with a degree that qualifies you to teach at some level. Teaching is fairly compatible with ongoing writing, in part because of the flexible hours, and if you get a chance to teach creative writing, the students who are motivated and talented will be a great source of inspiration for you. Even if you don't plan, or want, to teach, the program gives you a couple of years to apprentice yourself as a writer.

Obviously, a graduate program is only viable at certain points in your life. If you are currently the sole support of four children, it probably isn't a great idea at the moment, and that's okay. You don't need an advanced degree to write.

But I do recommend—strongly—that you spend some time in a formal, or semiformal, classroom setting. Most of us not only need to hear the basic rules—like "don't use clichés" and "get the story started right away"—repeated a few hundred times, we also need to have someone take a pencil and circle the place in the manuscript where we wrote the cliché, or mark off the paragraphs that have nothing to do with the story, before we're really able to do it for ourselves.

There's even more to it than that, though: There's a kind of magic that occurs when you are willing to take the risk of exhibiting your work-in-progress. It allows you to take the work to a new level, far beyond what mechanical advice people may have for you. That's because the process allows you more fully to imagine yourself in the role of the reader of your own material.

One-on-one instruction allows you to make this identification, but in a good writing group, the process is stepped up. As people in your group listen to each other discussing your work, it sparks more ideas in them. Then you can ask questions, and get a wide range of responses. Dissension is important, too; someone might have a complaint about, or praise of, your work that others don't share. The room crackles with your characters, your themes; you walk through it as though through an electrical storm, and get charged up all over again. This is as communal as writing novels ever gets.

After that your work begins to grow in a way that it hasn't before. This happens even though you will not agree with everything that others say about it, and they will not always be able to tell you exactly why something works or doesn't.

In your writing group, you will have the opportunity to read and critique others' work as well. At first you may not have a clue about what to say about it, but that will change. Critiquing other manuscripts isn't just the price you have to pay for the feedback you get; it's a genuine benefit to you, because you will be acquiring critical skills that will make your fiction better, too.

Writing Groups From Heaven

Thus the best situation is to be in an ongoing writer's group, one that meets regularly over an indefinite period and has a fairly steady core of members, although some turnover is inevitable, and also good.

It may take you a little while to find this group, and it's not a bad idea to spend six months or even a year in shorter-term classes. It's kind of like dating before marriage—you have to know what's out there. Those shorter-term classes will be a good way to find the ongoing groups, too: Often writing instructors will run private groups out of their homes. (Another way to find ongoing writing groups is to look for advertisements in alternative weeklies, those newspapers that are distributed free of charge in fine espresso bars everywhere.)

At a writers' conference, or in a limited-term class, people may only see one, and seldom more than three or four, samples of your writing. They have to go with their gut reactions to chapters taken out of context. In an ongoing group, however, everyone gets to read (or listen to) everyone else's work over a period of months and years. People may read entire drafts, or several entire drafts. They get to know your work almost as intimately as you do; their ears tune in to your melody, they pick up your rhythm; they come to understand what you are trying to do and what hurdles you have to overcome. They are motivated to give you as much help as possible, in part because they want it from you, and in part because you have all become colleagues.

This mutual, professional support and feedback is a far better system than showing your work to family and/or friends, which in fact, is no system at all.

In chapter three, I described how discussing your work-in-progress indiscriminately with others put you in a no-win situation. *Showing* them the work is even worse. The people close to you simply have too much at stake in not hurting your feelings or in figuring out what you wrote about them. If you sometimes think that the people in your writing group have personal agendas in tearing down or building up your writing, imagine how much more your wife does, when she may be worried that you're going to quit your job and let her support your newfound career.

Early on, I succumbed a couple of times to friends' requests to read what I had started working on, only to realize later that their interest was quite limited. They weren't unkind about what they read, but they couldn't help me with it, either; sometimes they didn't even bother to finish it. I was left feeling exposed, and even more uncertain than before, since what I had shown them had failed to arouse any great excitement.

But the bottom line is that *these people are not writers.* You might as well ask your boyfriend to peer into your mouth and give you his candid opinion of the new crown your dentist just put in.

In a disciplined, well-run writing group everyone knows just how important their own and everyone else's work is. People also know, or are in the process of learning, how to analyze a work of fiction. Ideally, after a shorter or longer period of class-hopping, you will find such a group of like-minded, right-thinking novelists who can become an emotional bulwark as well as the most effective source of the kind of serious criticism—and magic—we've been talking about.

Attitude Is Everything

What you must bring to the group (besides a pen) is a mix of humility, patience and resilience. Many would-be authors join their first groups expecting to be immediately recognized as geniuses. When that doesn't happen, they drop out. But the *will*-be authors stay in the group, and some of them become geniuses later.

Finding out that you aren't quite ready for Random House is a rite of passage, not a failure. If you can survive your first drubbing in a writing group and go back to the typewriter the next day, you are in fact a success.

After you suffer through your first critique, your initial reaction will probably be one of two extremes: Either you think that you need to do everything that everyone says exactly as he suggested, or you go home muttering, "Those jerks, they just didn't understand what I was trying to do."

Probably the truth is somewhere in between. That's why the best use that you can make of the feedback you get is to listen to it, write it down, and consider it over a period of time. This is another reason to write a first draft straight through: When you go back, you will have not only the writing, but the criticism in better perspective. Also, comments that you hear repetitively—"I still don't believe that George would be in love with Alice, she's just so mean"—will start to sink in.

Bad Apples and Sour Grapes

As high as I am on writing groups, I don't mean to suggest that they are all peaceful oases for the thirsty writer. No, unfortunately, writing groups attract fools, sadists and knuckle-crackers in only slightly less proportion than the population as a whole. There are some nasty groups out there, groups where people's faces are set aglow at the possibility that you really can't write and that they get to be the ones to tell you. You may bravely walk into a writing group, distribute copies of your first chapter, and wait for the magic to begin, only to have your first precious sentence dissected at great and cruel length.

If you have—or have had—a bad experience, put it behind you. There are, unfortunately, people who must immediately hone in on the faults of everyone else's work to dismiss it as a potential threat to their own. Don't hold the experience against all writing groups. Find a better group.

Most adult education programs or individual teachers will allow you to attend a first class or group meeting without further obligation, so you can see whether the experience level of the other students, the instructor's style, and the general vibes feel right to you. (Keep in mind that whatever your initial impressions, after a few meetings, your opinion may change.)

Some groups are mostly support-oriented. Members read aloud and other members frown earnestly and say things like, "Thank you for sharing your voice with us, Marie. I want to acknowledge you for that. By the way, was your father really fired from ten jobs in two years? How did you feel about that?" All of a sudden everyone is tearful about your parents, without another word to say about the infinitives you split. Everyone hugs you on the way out and that same earnest lady who began the discussion sniffs, "You really touched me. You brought up issues I need to work on." (You know the woman I mean, and somehow it will always get back to her issues.)

A good writing group should be supportive, but you need the criticism, too. The qualities you are looking for in a group, in fact, are not dissimilar to the ones that make a writers' conference good: An experienced leader and a group that's been around for a while are high on the list. At the first meetings you attend, ask yourself if the level of others' work and the comments offered will be a challenge to you. If you feel confident that you will be the best in the group and that others will be able to find no legitimate fault with your writing, what will you have to learn there? You will benefit from going into the hottest kitchen you can stand, a group of hardworking writers who are also tough critics.

Do your part, too. When you are critiquing others' work, be thorough, honest and fair. You are doing no kindness to someone to gloss over the flaws in his writing, still, everyone but racist pornographers deserve respect for the genuine effort they have made. Don't get too hung up on content, or at least offer your personal responses as just that—personal responses. Be as specific as possible. Offer suggestions and solutions when you can.

Only what the author has put on the page is up for discussion. Don't attempt to probe into the writer's motivations, as in, "Why do you want to write about such petty people?" or "Did you ever work as a high school principal?" It's irrelevant, and you only put people on the defensive that way. Stick to how you felt, reading what you read. "I had trouble liking these characters." "I didn't believe a high school principal would act this way."

As time goes by and you become more experienced, be tolerant of the newcomers who arrive. Remember that you were once as they are now.

Remember that in helping others make their books better, you are not helping the competition. The success of someone else's book does not lessen your chances for success; rather, any good book turns more people into readers and creates a bigger market for *every*one's books. You are helping to make this a more novel-friendly world.

A Group of One's Own

I urge you to seek out teachers you trust and admire. But I also realize that there will likely come a time when you want, or need, to form your own group.

There is an obvious advantage in that you get to participate in making the rules and choosing the other members. And if you live in a more isolated area, or have difficulty traveling for one reason or another, it may be the only practical way to go. (You may also just not have been able to find a good group that's already established.)

Here are some guidelines for forming your own writing group:

1. Decide at the first meeting how the group will operate and get the rules *in writing*.

2. Six to ten people is a good number. If there are fewer than six, flu season can wipe out meetings, and a couple of dropouts can cripple the group. Meanwhile, you are getting less input from fewer perspectives.

More than ten, though, and the group becomes unwieldy; meetings are long and the critiques will become repetitive. (People will begin their critiques by saying, "I pretty much agree with everything that's been said, so I won't repeat it," and then they'll repeat it.)

The perfect size will in some measure be dictated by how prolific the group members are. Everyone wants his or her chapters critiqued regularly, but few people want to read 300 pages of manuscript a week.

3. A "novels only" group is preferable, so you can all focus your energies on the refinements of that particular craft.

4. Weekly meetings are optimum. Meet at least every other week.

5. Decide how chapters will be read. You can photocopy and distribute them in advance of each meeting, so that members can mark them up and even read them a second time if they want. This is the more thorough method, but it's also more time-consuming (you'll have homework to do) and more expensive (because of the photocopying), so some groups decide that members will read their chapters aloud.

6. Determine how the critiques will be run. I recommend a first round during which time each member has ten minutes to deliver his or her critique on what he has read or heard (vary the order in which people deliver their critiques).

During that first round, the author must be silent. This is important. When being critiqued, otherwise timid writers can turn into William Jennings Bryan, defending their work as if it were the Bible, and objecting to any criticism, "That's in the next chapter!" This really wastes the group's time. *After* everyone has had his say, then the author should have a turn to explain anything, or ask more questions, or defend her work if she must (though it's still a waste of time), and then the others can add to or clarify their original comments.

7. Choose a leader. This doesn't have to be the most experienced writer or the best critic; in fact, you can rotate the position so that someone different has it each month. In an autonomous group, the role of leader isn't to be the teacher, it's to be the policeperson: to get the meeting started on time, to remind the author not to talk and the critiquers not to go on too long, etc. Sure, if you form the group, you can designate yourself leader. The reality is that some people are more committed than others, and one person is often the driving force behind a group. It's a dirty job, but someone has to do it.

8. Decide on a procedure for admitting new members. Group chemistry can be volatile, and this minimizes the territorialism that emerges when someone brings a new person to the group. You may decide in advance that you will ask prospective members to submit writing samples and then all vote on whether or not to admit them. Or you may feel comfortable with a more open-door policy that admits anyone with a good heart and an active typewriter.

9. Find a meeting place. It will generally be most convenient to meet at a member's house, but if you can find a free room at a local library, high school or church, or if you are a large and wealthy enough group to pool a few dollars to rent a room, then do so.

There are advantages to a classroom-style setting: You don't have to worry about the level of the roommate's CD player, and you don't have to reschedule when the host goes out of town. Also, the neutral surroundings will heighten the professional atmosphere.

Because that's what you want to be—professional. This is not a social gathering, it's a writing group. Don't let meetings degenerate into coffee klatches. When the meeting is over, then you can all go out for beer and pizza and grouse about how tough it is to be a writer, just like the nurses, legal secretaries and teachers.

Why "Network" Is Not a Dirty Word

I've indicated some of the advantages of a group dynamic when your work is discussed. But you do what you can, and you do what's best for you. If a writing group really doesn't work, because you live on a space station or because you've taken a vow of silence, or because you are genuinely phobic about having your work talked about in a group, exchange manuscripts with other writers by mail on a regular basis. You can either send each other written critiques, discuss the work over the phone, or both. Yet another alternative is to find a teacher or writing consultant and pay him or her to critique your work privately (yes, be prepared to pay).

People perpetuate the myth that writing can neither be taught nor learned when they smirk, "Well, the great writers never went to graduate school. They just wrote." But the fact is that "great" writers, whoever we decide they are—the list would certainly include Hemingway, Fitzgerald, Faulkner, Flaubert, Conrad, Tolstoy, Dostoyevski and a few thousand others—were almost all plugged into networks of other writers and editors with whom to share their work and from whom to get feedback.

Admittedly, these great writers of yore had an advantage in that even though they were doing it, they didn't use the terms "networking" or "feedback." The former word is particularly irksome, in that it makes one think of yuppies in hot pink spandex carrying heavy Filofaxes and promising to call you back later, usually from their cars.

Nevertheless, whether you're looking for a good writers' conference, an ongoing group or an agent, networking can get you there. Make it your personal verb. Networking, you see, means not just asking, "Do you know a good writing class?" but pressing on, in the face of a negative response, to "Do you know anyone else who might know a class, or do you know someone who might know someone who might know a class?" This gets you beyond the limits of your own circle, into Real Networking. Spandex is optional.

TO GET THAT NOVEL STARTED

Find people with whom you can start. Find people who will keep you going.

How to Be Your Own Grandmother

The Noodge

My grandmother was an intelligent, hardworking and good-hearted woman who wanted the people she loved to be successful and happy. She was also the *noodge* of the century.

"Noodge" is a Yiddish word that, like many Yiddish words, eludes precise translation. Roughly, to noodge is to nag, or to pester, but it often implies nagging or pestering someone to do something for his or her own good.

My grandmother did not want me to be a novelist; a lawyer would have been much more like it. Later, when it became clear I was not destined for fame as a litigator, she started on me about selling real estate. "You have to go where the people are," she would say, meaning, "Sitting at a typewriter in your living room — *this* is a way to meet men?" Well, it wasn't a good way to meet men, but it was what I wanted to do.

Finally, my grandmother accepted that, and once she did, she noodged me about writing, because after all, if I was going to be a novelist, then I had better actually be one, and not just talk about it. "I hope your book is coming along," she would remark weightily. There was more reproach than hope in it, though; my grandmother was not an orthopedic-shod, smell-the-cookies-and-smile granny in a blue-and-white polka-dot dress. Plenty of blintzes and pans of chicken breasts came out of her kitchen, but her ambitions for us were far more complex than our keeping warm, dry and fed.

I often got annoyed with my grandmother when she noodged me to wear lipstick, lose weight, or to join one of those singles' groups for which bad skin and a nervous, nasal laugh are requirements of membership. At my most frustrated, though, I always knew that she was deeply concerned with what happened to me, and now that she's gone, I wish she was here so that we could fight about what my children, her great-grandchildren, are wearing and eating, and what they will do when they grow up.

The Noodge Inside Us All

When my grandmother passed away I inherited her crown (noodginess is a quality that skips generations). It is my duty, then, as reigning *noodge*, to seek out those who would become novelists and give them a hard time until they do.

Of course, many years before she died I internalized my grandmother's noodginess the way I internalized aspects of the Beast. So, along with the voice that tells me *not* to write, to give up, and to make way for talents greater than my own, there's another voice, gloomily rhetorical and a little sarcastic: "Are you planning to write today, Donna? Is this what a writer does — her laundry?"

Yes, she's still as annoying as heck, but the Noodge is my ally. The Noodge has decided that writing a novel is the most important thing in the world, something so important that you wouldn't question it any more than you'd question the Bill of Rights or the fundamental healthiness of milk and sunshine, no matter what those newfangled studies say.

You have a Noodge, too, although you might prefer to call it something else — the Friend, the Teacher, even the Boss. I don't think any of them say it better that Noodge, because Noodge is neither buddy nor slave driver. What the Noodge does is keep you on the hook. The Noodge wants you to write, to complete, and to publish "that" novel and to move on to the next. The Noodge will stand over you, deprive herself of sleep, food and even air, to make sure you get your writing done. If you don't, the implied threat is that the Noodge will jump off the nearest bridge or at the very least weep herself silly.

Let me assure you that no amount of genius you may have been blessed with will substitute for a good, bullying Noodge in four-inch heels and red lipstick, folding her arms under her corseted bosom and reminding you, "I don't see that you've done a-a-n-n-y writing today! No dessert until you do!"

Often you will want your Noodge to go away. A lot of books were written in the 70s telling you how to send her packing so you could love yourself and do your own thing. But if you tried the self-help books and they didn't work, you are fortunate.

Good people in your life will noodge you — good teachers, good writers in your writing group, and the family and friends who believe in what you're doing. Leonard Bishop, at over six feet and with a linebacker's shoulders, has been the Noodge personified to many novelists.

But you need to become your own Noodge, too. Love yourself, discipline yourself, and don't apologize for wanting to succeed. "Artists" may hold forth self-righteously about their wish to enlighten others, but if you want to write, that's all you need to know, and you don't need to justify that to me, to yourself, or to anyone else. You don't need to pretend that it's only for the good of humanity that you would accept being interviewed by *People* magazine.

The Challenges Remain

During the period when I was just beginning to feel my way to the typewriter, I attended a panel discussion in which I heard several authors complain that their agents didn't cut them big enough deals, and that their publishers didn't promote their books enough, and that Joe and Josephine Citizen didn't read anyway because they were too busy renting videos.

God, I thought, *I can't wait to have these problems!* I couldn't imagine that, having once published, I would ever doubt myself or my work again, or that, in my new exalted state, a contract dispute or the neglect of the public would trouble me.

Well, in fact, being published is one of the top four best things that ever happened to me. Still, now I understand what the authors on this panel discussion were talking about. Now I understand that the struggle continues—not just to market one's work, but to find ways and a reason to write.

In *The Writing Life*, Annie Dillard describes the truth all novelists must face:

> . . . your work is so meaningless, so fully for yourself alone, and so worthless to the world, that no one but you cares whether you do it well, or ever. . . . There are many manuscripts already—worthy ones, most edifying and moving ones, intelligent and powerful ones. . . . Why not shoot yourself, actually, rather than finish one more excellent manuscript on which to gag the world?

I don't know why you don't shoot yourself, but you don't. Instead, every day you begin again, reinvent yourself, return patiently to the act of conjuring a story with people in it from the darkness of your own mind. For it to read as if it flowed effortlessly from your unconscious, you must eke it out a word at a time, and then change many of those words. You don't know if it will ever be any good, so you decide not to think about that.

So the challenges remain, and the struggle goes on. What happens, though, is that doing the work becomes the goal. When the work is finished, published or not (yes, published is better), it's on its own, and you're writing something else.

The point of all this is that since you never arrive at a place where writing is always easy, fun or secure, you might as well start enjoying the ups and downs of the process now, even as you set out.

Some Final Thoughts You Already Know

Novels last a long time; the good ones don't go bad. They don't need electricity, and there's no static or commercials. They don't talk back, beat you at handball, forget to take out the garbage, or spit up. You can carry them around with you, put them down in the middle of a sentence, and pick them up again whenever you want. They're always there, waiting for you.

But you and I already know what miracles novels are. That's why we want to write them. Just as we have our favorites—the stories that seem part of our own pasts—so we want to shape new stories that will become precious to others. That's all the "artistic" rationale you'll ever need.

So in the writing of your novels, I wish you luck, but more than that I wish you stamina, persistence and faith. I wish you a novel that sings to you so loudly that it wakes you in the night, a novel you can love. I wish you many such novels, and much happy writing.

So get that novel started, already.

INDEX